How to Study

Practical Tips for University Students

PHIL RACE

Blackwell
Publishing

350 Main Street, Malden, MA 02148-5020, USA
108 Cowley Road, Oxford OX4 1JF, UK
550 Swanston Street, Carlton, Victoria 3053, Australia

First published 2003 by Blackwell Publishing Ltd

Library of Congress Cataloging-in-Publication Data
Race, Philip.
   How to study : practical tips for university students / Phil Race.
      p. cm.
Includes bibliographical references and index.
   ISBN 1-4051-0693-X (pbk. : alk. paper)
   1. Study skills. I. Title.

LB2395.R34 2003
371.3′028′1—dc21

2003005889

A catalogue record for this title is available from the British Library.

Set in 10/12.5 Baskerville
by SetSystems Ltd, Saffron Walden, Essex
Printed and bound in the United Kingdom
TJ International, Padstow, Cornwall

For further information on
Blackwell Publishing, visit our website:
http://www.blackwellpublishing.com

How to Study

Contents

Part III   Essays

Part IV   Presentations

Part V   Ups and Downs

Part VI   Revision – Getting Your Act Together

Part VII   Exams – Before, During and After!

Part VIII   Job Hunting

About this Book

Welcome to this book, which is intended to make sure that you become a successful student. I've written this book to be a companion to you on your journey through college years, and to help you learn from other people's experience, and to save you time. It was way back in 1992 that I published the original *500 Tips for Students.* I dedicated it 'to my son Angus, in the hope that he may read the advice that he won't listen to'! I'm delighted to report that he did, and now has both a BSc and an MSc. The present book contains a great deal more – since 1992 I've learned all sorts about the help which you may need! This new book focuses much more strongly on what will be your main agenda – doing yourself justice with coursework and exams, then going on to apply for jobs effectively, efficiently and successfully.

Since 1992, I've divided my time between helping students to improve their learning tactics, and helping lecturers develop their teaching tactics. The common factor is assessment, and the additional experience I've gained from helping lecturers to devise and implement assessment is crammed into this book, so that *you* can maximize your own performance in the various kinds of assessment you will meet.

Your academic success depends not so much on how much you know, but on how well you show what you know in exams and coursework assessments. There are many ways in which you can put this book to work for you, including:

- dipping into it selectively, for whatever is important to you at a particular moment in your studies;

- working through it systematically, looking for the parts that are most directly relevant to your own situation as a student;
- experimenting with ideas you've not yet tried out for yourself, and finding out which ideas really work well for you;
- using it to find out to what extent your existing study tactics are already fit for purpose in the context of your present studying;
- using it as a basis for developing even better ideas of your own.

Part I, 'Managing your Learning', offers a range of suggestions, the most important ones probably being on 'Managing your time' and 'Getting started'! Then Part II looks at how to make the most of lectures, handouts, practical work, open learning materials and computers, as well as how best to reflect on your learning when you need to, for example if you're asked to build a portfolio or learning log. Part III homes in on 'Essays', from planning them to getting them back with feedback. It ends with some suggestions about how to cite other people's work in your own essays. Part IV is about 'Presentations', and will help to take the fear away from the task of preparing one and giving it – and will also pave the way towards you becoming better at handling interview questions. Part V is called 'Ups and Downs', and is about handling some of the more difficult moments you may encounter as a student. Part VI is about 'Revision – Getting Your Act Together', and aims at not only helping you to revise really effectively, but also to make it all more efficient, so that your life isn't ruined by revision. Part VII is called 'Exams – Before, During and After!' This offers practical, tried-and-tested suggestions to help you to get more marks, and to have a better experience of exams in general. Finally, Part VIII on 'Job Hunting' will help you to write and maintain an effective curriculum vitae (CV), and apply systematically and logically for jobs, and put your best foot forward at interviews.

However, all the tips in the world will only help you if you put them into practice. At the end of the day, it's up to you. But this book will help you with how best to go about your studies, and explain why it's worth you investing in your skills at being an effective student.

I'm really grateful to many people – students and staff – for countless valuable suggestions that have increased the value of this book to you. In particular, Professor Sally Brown discussed many aspects of the book with me during its creation, and Professor John Cowan, Dr Clara Davies and Chris Butcher offered wise suggestions that helped me to develop a number of parts of the book.

Finally, may I wish you good luck! You shouldn't *need* luck if you develop your skills towards being a really effective student, but luck is not a bad thing.

Phil Race

Part I

Managing Your Learning

Wanting to Learn

If you're already completely fired up about being a student, and your motivation is beyond question, you probably don't need these tips. But few of us *remain* fired up permanently, and it can be useful to find ways of re-enthusing yourself from time to time – especially when things start to get that bit harder in your studies.

1. **Factors underpinning successful learning.** In my own work researching how people learn best, I've asked countless people about how they learnt things successfully – and what has gone wrong in their learning too. Their replies indicate five main factors underpinning successful learning:

   - **wanting** to learn;
   - **needing** to learn;
   - **learning by doing**: practice, repetition, learning from mistakes;
   - learning from feedback: other people's reactions, praise, criticism;
   - **making sense** of what's been learned – 'digesting' it, getting your head round it.

   In this book, there are many practical tips to help you take control over how *you* make the most of these five factors.

2. **Links between various processes.** There are various ways of thinking about how the various processes involved in

learning something successfully connect with each other. The five factors listed above (in point 1 above) all affect each other, in fact. When you *want* to learn something (or *need* to learn it), nothing much happens until you *do* something – some practice, trial and error, and repetition perhaps. But it's then important to *make sense* of what you've done, to deepen your learning. This is best done when you can get *feedback* on what you've done. The feedback helps to clarify what you still need to learn, and how best to go about some further practice, and so on.

3. **Imagine having a barometer recording how much you *want* to learn.** This barometer would naturally show quite different readings on successive days. It would vary quite a lot depending on exactly what you were learning at the time. It's quite useful to keep track mentally of which aspects of your studies read high on wanting to learn, and which (more

importantly) could be areas of low pressure. These are the areas that are going to need your attention sooner or later.

4. **Rank your subjects in order of how much you feel that you want to learn them.** This will vary quite a lot from week to week, but it's always useful to *know* how it's varying. In short, the subjects that rank highest in your 'want to learn' stakes will tend to look after themselves, as you'll easily manage to find the time to do what you need to do when learning them. The subjects that repeatedly come out towards the bottom of your 'want to learn' list are potential danger areas. You may indeed *need* to learn them effectively alongside the rest.

5. **Plan to spend a little time most days on subjects you don't particularly want to learn.** This is investing in your future success. Your reward strategy can be to spend the *next* period of study on something you're really interested in, feeling all the better because you've already tackled something less stimulating and done something useful (however small) with it.

6. **Make a list of 'what's in it for you' overall.** Think ahead to the next stage of your life, after you will have finished your present studies. What are the pay-offs you'll reap then, as a result of the hard work you put in now? It can help you to maintain your motivation if now and then you remind yourself of some good reasons for putting in that extra bit of effort now.

7. **Talk to fellow-students about why they're studying.** Ask your friends what keeps them going when the going gets tough. You may even find it useful to adopt some of their reasons for putting in some effort with their studies. Or indeed, if you find that you already have better reasons for wanting to learn than theirs, you could justly feel pleased with yourself.

8. **Analyse what can enhance your own 'want' to do things.** What sort of rewards work for you? The more you can understand what drives you successfully, the better you can fine-tune your ways of studying.

9. **When there's something you definitely *don't* want to learn, work out why this is so.** What is it about the subject

that turns you off? Or is it to do with the teacher? Is it that
you just don't *like* a particular teacher? At the end of the day,
we don't have to like all of our teachers – we can still learn
from people we don't like. Obviously it's more fun learning
from people we like, but we can't have this luxury all the time.

10. **Be a little careful with things you *really* want to learn.**
While it's always good to feel highly motivated about learning
something, keep an eye on where the goalposts are. The
biggest danger can be spending too much time and energy
learning something you're really enjoying, when it doesn't
actually count for very much in terms of marks or grades or
credit towards the qualification you're aiming at.

Needing to Learn

In the previous set of tips, we've explored some ways of keeping tabs on how much you *want* to learn different things in your studies. Now let's look more closely at the other side of the continuum – things you don't particularly want to learn, but which you do indeed *need* to learn. You'll always have both kinds of things on your learning agenda, and keeping your balance between the two is part of the art of being a successful learner.

1. **Find all you can about exactly *what* you need to learn.** This makes it a lot easier, and saves you time, not least sparing you from wasting time and energy learning all sorts of things you *don't* actually need to learn.

2. **Get into the habit of really *using* intended learning outcomes.** Your subject syllabus will almost certainly be expressed in terms of such intended outcomes. They're sometimes called 'objectives'. You may find these listed in a course handbook, for example. They are often written along the lines: 'By the end of this module, students will be able to . . .', followed by a list of the things you will be expected to be able to do to *demonstrate* that you've achieved the learning outcomes.

3. **Find out even more about those intended learning outcomes.** In particular, how are they linked to assessment? One way or another, the extent to which *you* achieve the intended learning outcomes will be assessed in due course.

The more you know about what you've got to do to *show* that you've achieved the outcomes, the better you can work out priorities for what you need to learn.

4. **Think about *why* you need to learn things.** There are usually good reasons. It's often the case that getting to grips with topic A is necessary before you can master topic B and so on. Even if topic A seems quite boring or useless to you at the time, if you *know* why you need to spend some time and energy on it, you're much better geared up to tackle it.

5. **Keep tabs on your progress with things you need to learn.** This helps you to see that even those topics which you don't particularly *want* to learn can be quite manageable. It can be reassuring to make a list of things you did because you knew you *needed* to do them, and gradually reduce the number of things remaining on your *need to learn* agenda.

6. **Where you can, turn a 'need' into a 'want'.** You can't always do this of course. But sometimes you can find yourself good reasons for wanting to learn something that you need to learn in any case. Sometimes you can work out further ways in which the thing you need to learn will help you with other things in your life.

7. **Make lists of the things you need to do.** You can put such a list up on your wall as a reminder. Have one column for the tasks, and another column for the 'need to do this before' date, and a third column to tick when you've done things. There are few things more satisfying than putting ticks in this third column – or indeed looking at a list of things you've completely finished doing.

8. **Extend the 'need to' lists to other areas of your life.** Don't just focus on the things you need to learn or on study tasks you need to do. Include some of the other things which need to be done, such as contacting a friend, replying to a letter or email, getting something at the supermarket and so on. This helps you to do your planning about studying alongside the normal everyday planning about living. It's always better if studying takes its place as part of your whole life, rather than being something separate that you sometimes do.

Learning by Doing

A great many of the suggestions in this book are about *doing* things. Not much learning actually happens if you don't do things. In the present set of tips, let's look at 'learning by doing' in a global way.

1. **Accept that not much happens if you do nothing!**
   Einstein is reported to have said, 'Knowledge is experience, everything else is just information.' Experience is about doing things. Your lecture notes and textbooks and web sources won't magically turn themselves into knowledge in your brain without you *doing* something with the information they contain.

2. **Beware of *thinking about doing* something for too long, rather than actually *doing* it.** While it is very sensible to plan what you're going to do, a danger is that it can be *easier* to sit there planning than actually getting round to starting to do something. Make yourself a rule that you're only going to plan anything for a few minutes, and then you'll spend at least the next few minutes starting to do even just one of the things you've been planning.

3. **Some kinds of doing have greater learning pay-off than others.** For example, you don't actually learn very much at all if you just sit and read and read and read. Most of what you read just evaporates from your mind. But if you make summaries as you read, or jot down questions as you read, or discuss and argue about what you read with other people, your learning pay-off is far higher.

4. **You don't have to finish everything you start.** Some
    people feel that they've let themselves down if they start
    something and don't carry on there and then till they finish it.
    However, the important thing is to get started. Once you've
    started something, it's a lot easier to *resume* it later than it was
    to start it. You do indeed need a little self-discipline to return
    to things which you've already started and finish them off
    when needed, but that is relatively easy to cultivate.

5. **Doing doesn't have to be boring.** There are hundreds
    of different sorts of things you can do, all of which have
    learning pay-off. This book is full of suggestions about what
    you can do.

6. **There are two main categories of things you can do.**
    One is 'things you *have* to do in any case', such as coursework
    tasks which are going to be assessed, practical work, and so on.
    The other category is 'things you can choose for yourself to
    do', including (not least) keeping on top of the work you've
    already done, revising for exams, and exploring on your own
    initiative interesting aspects of your syllabus.

7. **Variety is the spice of learning by doing.** When you've got
    a substantial menu of possible learning-by-doing activities, it's
    easy to ring the changes so that you're not doing just one kind
    of thing for too long at a time.

8. **Some things can be done in minutes.** For example,
    making a summary of 'three important points to remember
    from last Tuesday's 10 o'clock lecture' could be done in five
    minutes or less. That summary in turn would be a useful
    learning tool to keep those important points in mind, and to
    use again for later revision.

9. **Some things take longer.** Writing an essay or report takes
    longer. Writing a project report or dissertation takes longer
    still. But nothing has to be done all in one sitting; even the
    biggest tasks are best done a little at a time.

10. **Some things can be done almost anywhere.** For example,
    you can *think* wherever you are. You can choose to think for
    five minutes about what you already know about topic X,
    wherever you are, if you have five minutes to spare.

11. **Some things can only be done in certain places.** For
    example, if you're writing a report with a word processor, you

need to be at a machine to do that. But that doesn't stop you doing related tasks in other places, for example *planning* the report, *editing* your first draft, *researching* things to include in your report, and so on.

Learning from Feedback

Feedback is important. You'll get lots of feedback, and this can really deepen your learning. But you need to be *looking* for feedback to get the most from it. And you need to be *receptive* to it when you get it. The following tips will help you make the most of feedback.

1. **Regard *all* feedback as valuable.** Whether feedback is in the form of praise or criticism, you will get a lot more out of it if you value it.
2. **Feedback from *anyone* is useful.** While it's understandable to regard the feedback you get from lecturers and tutors as authoritative, you will also get feedback all the time from fellow students, and other people around you.
3. **Don't shrug off positive feedback.** When you're complimented on your work, there's a temptation to try to ease any feeling of embarrassment by saying 'Well, it's not *so* special really', and so on. The problem with doing this is that *you* then start to believe this. It's much better to allow yourself to swell with pride, at least for a little while. This helps you to accept the positive feedback, and to build upon it and do even better next time, perhaps.
4. **Practise thanking people for their positive feedback.** Simply saying 'thanks, I'm glad you liked that' can be enough sometimes. When people are thanked for giving you praise or compliments, they're more likely to do so again, and this means more and better feedback for you.

5. **Don't get defensive when feedback is critical.** It's perfectly natural to try to protect yourself from the hurt of critical feedback, but the problem then is that this interferes with the flow of critical feedback to you. The more you can gently probe for even more feedback, the more useful the feedback turns out to be.

6. **Thank people for critical feedback too.** Even when you're not pleased with the critical feedback you've just received, it can be useful to say something along the lines of 'Well, thanks for telling me about this, it should be useful for me in future', and so on.

7. **Don't just wait for feedback, ask for it.** Don't lose any opportunities to press gently for even more feedback than you already have received. Ask questions, such as 'What do you think was the best thing I did here?' and 'What would be the most useful change I could make next time I do something similar?' and so on.

Making Sense of Things – 'Digesting'

In some respects, this is the most important of the processes underpinning successful learning. When you've made sense of something, you've deepened your understanding of it, and you're in a better position to *show* that your learning has been successful. Many suggestions in other parts of this book are about making sense of what you're learning, but the following tips should help you get started on this.

1. **Don't just accumulate information.** You can have in your possession all the right books, articles, handouts and websites, but not yet have got your head round the information they contain. To start making sense of anything, you've got to *do* something with it. There are all sorts of actions you can choose from – here are just a few key ones: summarize it, explain it to someone else, apply it, turn it into some questions to test yourself on, solve problems with it, and so on.

2. **Don't worry *too* much about understanding things at first.** Quite often, we need to live with an idea or a concept for quite some time before the light really dawns. Meanwhile, however, we can still be *doing* things with it, as above, paving the way for the light to dawn in due course.

3. **Keep track of what you've made sense of.** One problem is that sometimes when we've made sense of something, it seems like a good stopping place in our thinking, and we can easily 'lose it' again.

4. **Use feedback to help you to make sense of things.** Sometimes it is only when other people give feedback on what we've done that we can see which parts we have successfully digested, and which parts were not yet understood.

5. **Explain things you've just learned to other people.** The act of putting an idea into words and explaining it to someone else is one of the best ways of understanding it. Anyone will do – or at least anyone who is prepared to listen to you. Even better, of course, is someone who knows something about the subject already – particularly someone else who is learning it.

6. **Explain things to yourself!** When you can't take the opportunity to practise explaining what you've just learned to other people, try mentally telling yourself all about it. This is still useful to you, as it is a rehearsal for what you'll need to do later on, for example in exams. It helps you to get the ideas more clearly sorted out in your own mind, and sometimes alerts you to things you need to research a bit further until you get a grip on them.

Taking Charge of
Your Studies

Who's in charge of *your* learning? At school, your answer might well have been 'the teachers!' At home, it could have been 'parents!' Perhaps parents are still nagging you to study harder? You probably already know that it's only when we do things for ourselves that we really get going, and this set of tips might help you to take a greater sense of *ownership* of your studying. If *you* are in the driving seat of your studying, you're much more likely to get somewhere. So here goes...

1. **Why are you studying?** Make sure that you have several good answers to this question. It's best to be studying because you *want* to study, not because other people expect you to. It helps to look ahead to what's in it for you when your studies have been successful – better job prospects, more interesting career choices, a better life altogether. It's *your* life; you're investing your time and energy in *your* future.

2. **Who are the people driving your learning?** Lecturers will be included here, but they can't do your learning for you – they've done theirs already. Parents or brothers or sisters or friends may still feel as though they're trying to drive your learning, but they can't take your exams for you! Try to rationalize other people's actions as *supporting* your learning, not driving it. Be your own driver.

3. **Who are you trying to be like?** Many students feel themselves to be following in the footsteps of others who have gone before. No harm in this, but you don't really want to

follow those footsteps through every patch of nettles and into every boggy bit. It's useful to learn from others' experiences, but important to make studying *your* experience.

4. **Set your own targets.** Sometimes it will feel as though everyone is setting targets for you – lecturers, tutors, even fellow students. Yes, you'll have to meet other people's targets, but there's nothing to stop you setting your own targets too – for example, set your own deadlines a few days or weeks *ahead* of the targets they give you.

5. **Become your own assessor.** In due course, your work will be assessed by lecturers and examiners. But you're the *first* person to see your work. If you make yourself skilled at assessing it as you do it, you'll pick up a lot of marks which you otherwise could have thrown away carelessly. But you've got to *want* to be able to self-assess your work, so start thinking about this as one of the targets you choose to aim towards.

6. **Become a clue collector!** All the time, you'll be getting clues about what you're *really* expected to be doing as you study. Such clues come in your lectures, in course handbooks, in task briefings, and of course are made quite plain in past exam questions. Don't just notice these clues and then forget about them – store them up in your notes. You could even start a little pocket notebook for 'must remember that' ideas about what will gain you extra credit in your studies.

7. **Decide that you're going to make the most of feedback on your learning.** This is easy enough when tutors write 'very good' on your essays or reports, but harder when they write 'you didn't address the question . . .', and so on. Remember that all feedback is useful, and can help you in future work. But feedback only really works if you *want* it – don't just wait for it to land on you.

8. **Make plans and change them often.** It takes more guts to change a plan than to make one. It's not a sign of weakness to abandon a plan that just isn't working out. You'll get better and better at planning by noticing which of your plans run smoothly, and which need adjusting.

9. **Regard everything and everyone as your resources.** All the people around you can be learnt from – even if sometimes it's just a matter of learning what *not* to do yourself. All the

course materials, textbooks, web pages, handouts and notes are *your* resources; some will be much more useful than others, of course, but you'll soon get skilled at working out which ones to focus upon.

10. **Don't imagine that you can study all the time.** No one can. Brains can't work day and night like computers. The important thing is to become more efficient at studying, more effective at focusing on tasks, and better at taking time out from studying with an easy conscience because you know that you're doing enough.

Managing Your Time

Only you can do this. It's *your* time. We've all got exactly the same amount of time to manage in a day – 24 hours – yet some people seem rushed and other people seem laid back. It's better being laid back about time, especially when you know that you *deserve* to be laid back. That's your reward for tackling your time management head on.

1. *Decide* **that you're in charge of your time.** This doesn't mean that you're going to sit back and waste it, but it also doesn't mean you're going to get so flustered about all the different things you need to do that you end up doing nothing much but scrabble around. Being in charge of your time is about making sure that you get good value from using it.
2. **Remind yourself what's in it for you.** Being good at time management will improve your quality of life. You'll be more efficient, more effective, and under a lot less pressure from other people.
3. **Managing time *makes* time.** Yes, it *takes* some time too, but the hours you'll save by getting good at time management will be *your* time to do what you want to with.
4. **Get a degree in time management!** You won't see these listed in any prospectus, but just about all degrees depend on being an accomplished time-manager. The better you are at using your study time well, the more likely you will be to get whatever qualifications you want.

5. **Think in terms of high learning pay-off.** Choose to use
    your time to do things that have high learning pay-off, such as
    making summaries of things, discussing things with others,
    quizzing yourself about what you've just learnt, quizzing
    yourself about what you learnt three days ago, and three weeks
    ago, and so on.

6. **Limit the time you spend on things with low learning
    pay-off.** There's less learning gain per minute in tasks such as
    passive reading, writing essays, writing reports, doing practical
    work, and simply sitting in some of the less stimulating
    lectures. You've still *got* to do these things, of course, but don't
    kid yourself that you're getting a lot into your mind just
    because you're busy doing them.

7. **Don't waste time *thinking* about doing some work.** We're
    all very good at putting off the evil moment of actually *starting*
    work. Just start – that's saved you from wasting any time
    putting it off.

8. **Manage your minutes, and the hours will look after
    themselves.** Don't wait till you've got a good, solid, quiet
    three hours to get on with your next bit of studying – you

haven't got such a time window! Use what you've got, five minutes now, five minutes soon, and lots and lots of short-but-useful spells of time.

9. **Spend some of the short bits of time on *your* learning agendas.** For example, it takes just a few minutes to look over the notes from one of last week's lectures, or make your own summary of something you've read, or prepare a checklist of things you're going to do in the next few hours or days.

10. **Choose to use the *first* 10% of the time available for a task.** You'll probably have noticed that, left to human nature, we usually manage to finish a task well enough in the *last* 10% of the available time. It's pure logic that just as much could have been done in the *first* 10%. Think of all the other things you can then get through in the remaining 90% of the available time for that task – not least spending a little time now and then going back to the task and polishing it up. That means more marks; if it's an assessed task – a lot more marks.

11. **Set your own deadlines.** Your lecturers will set you deadlines, but make *yours* earlier ones – much earlier ones. Set staged deadlines as well as final deadlines. Break big tasks into manageable chunks.

12. **Tell other people about your targets and deadlines.** Knowing that they could then ask you, 'Have you done what you said you were going to do by today?' is a great incentive to making sure you're going to be able to reply, 'Of course, yes.'

13. **Be an early person.** Don't just turn up on time for lectures, tutorials, practicals, and so on, but get there that bit early. Even if you're standing around doing nothing as a result, you can use your brain to do some useful thinking. You can tune in to what you already know about the topic, and what you want to find out about the topic, and how that topic relates to other things you're learning – all 'high learning pay-off' thinking. This is far better than being late, when most of your brain would be full of thoughts about being late!

14. **Get ahead of schedule.** Try to get yourself a couple of weeks (or more) ahead of where you need to be. It's a great insurance policy. You won't then be completely thrown by the unexpected – a bout of 'flu, the sudden family crisis, a friend who needs your time, and so on. It's a great feeling when

you've got time in hand. You then don't use up energy worrying about hand-in dates, assessment dates or exam timetables, and can use your energy instead for gaining learning pay-off.

15. **Keep going backwards.** Make time to stop and reflect. Go back to what you learnt yesterday, the day before, the week before, and so on. You still need all of this. Don't just go surging forwards, letting all of your learning evaporate in your wake. Consolidate. You're measured sooner or later on how much you've consolidated – not on how much you once learnt then forgot!

16. **Plan time off.** When you're ahead of schedule, you deserve some time off. When you take *planned* time off, you've got a clear conscience and can *enjoy* the time off far more than if you'd just escaped from the pressure of a backlog of work. Enjoying time off restores your brain and body, and makes you fitter for your next bout of high pay-off learning.

Getting Started

This is about task management, over and above time management. Suppose you've got something important to do in your studying: if you don't *start* it, you certainly won't finish it! Human nature seems to dictate that the harder the task, the easier it is to postpone starting it. Once started, however, most tasks get done, and they often get done far more quickly and comfortably than we ever imagined. These tips are in two parts: first, looking at the enemies of task management – those 'work-avoidance strategies we can fall prey to – and then at how to *really* get started when you decide to do it.

Check out your work-avoidance strategies: do any of these below apply to you? If not, well done. If they do, however, know your enemy, and do something about them.

1. **Doing all sorts of tidying up before you start?** For example, tidying your desk, tidying your room, tidying your flat, tidying the town? By all means do a little tidying *after* you've done half an hour on the task (if, that is, you still want to). At least then you'll still be thinking about what you did in that half-hour as you tidy up.
2. **Doing easy little tasks, so as to put off getting started on harder bigger ones?** This one's easy to put right: just do half an hour straightaway on the bigger one, then spend a little time on one or two of the easier ones to catch your

breath mentally. You'll be surprised just how much of that big task you got done in just half an hour, anyway, and it's no longer in the realm of the 'unstarted'.

3. **Indulging in displacement activities?** Doing your laundry? Ironing your socks? Going off on a food shop? Oiling your bike? Oiling everyone else's bikes? There are enough displacement activities available to you to fill a book twice as big as this one! Don't kid yourself – you're not likely to invent any new ones. They've all been done before. And they've always had the same effect – slowing people down from doing important things. All of these displacement activities have their proper place – *after* the important task is well under way, when you can keep your brain full of important stuff while you potter around with easy stuff.

4. **Collecting all the bits and pieces you may need to do the important task?** Getting together all of the books, papers, handouts, notes? Getting together pens, pencils, drawing instruments? You seldom need *everything* just to get started on the task. Once it's under way, you can rest your brain by doing a little more collecting.

5. **Getting things just right to start?** Sorting out what's on your computer. Filing everything properly in folders. Backing up important stuff on floppies. Answering that email you've not replied to yet. All useful stuff, of course, but far better to do it as *time out* once the big task is under way.

Tactics for really getting started on a task: choose from the list below those actions that will really help *you*. Better still, this is where you *can* be inventive: invent some even better ones of your own. For the purposes of discussion, imagine you'd been set an essay to write (but you can easily extend the ideas below to all sorts of other important tasks).

---

1. **Get out two pieces of blank paper.** Don't now walk for two hours looking for a shop that's still open to *buy* some paper – the back of a handout will do for this. Some things one can do straight onto a computer, but other things still

need paper. (This is not least because once you've powered up your computer, there will be yet more displacement activities open to you. If it's logged on to the net, there's the whole Internet to surf! At the very least there'll be a game or two on the machine.) Furthermore, you can stick useful bits of paper on the wall when you work later on your computer, to remind you about what you're actually doing.

2. **Jot down what you already know about the topic.** On one blank sheet of paper, put down the topic title or keywords from the task briefing in an oval about the size of an egg in the middle of the page, draw 'spokes' radiating round the egg, and write something you already know (just a word or two to remind you) at the end of each spoke. Be free-ranging with your egg diagram. Hatch your thoughts, don't just keep them cooped up in your brain.

3. **Jot down what you don't yet know about the topic.** 'Sorry, *what?*' Use another blank sheet of paper, again with the topic in an egg in the middle. This time draw spokes with *questions* at the ends of them – questions relating to things that you don't yet know about the topic, but might need to find out.

4. **Now look once again, very carefully, at the task instructions.** Look for the keywords in the instructions. What exactly have you been asked to do? Is it 'discuss', or 'describe', or 'compare and contrast' or 'evaluate' or 'find out' and so on? Look again at what you know and don't-yet-know, and check out which things are really relevant to the task as asked.

5. **Phone a friend? Talk to other people if they're there?** These egg diagrams of what you know and don't yet know are even better if you do them with a friend or two. This isn't copying. This isn't cheating. It's just thinking together, and enriching everyone's 'ideas bank'. There will always be things or questions that you wouldn't have thought of just sitting on your own.

6. **Now start prioritizing.** What's most important in the various things you already know? Which are the most important questions among the things you don't yet know? What do you really, really need to find out? Go round both egg diagrams

putting the things on the ends of the spokes in order of
importance. Put brackets around the things that didn't turn
out to be important. You *could* cross them out or erase them
forever, but it's sometimes useful to keep them as a record of
ideas you thought about briefly then discounted.

7.   **Now start on the task itself.** Don't start at the beginning
     necessarily, but just start. Put something down on paper (or
     compose something on the computer) that will be a rough
     draft of one small part of the bigger task. *Then* you can
     happily spend a little time doing one or two of that mountain
     of other things you might have still been doing if you hadn't
     been so wise as to have already started. But strangely enough,
     most of the displacement activities won't seem nearly as
     attractive to you as they were *before* you started the real task.

Take Charge of Your Syllabus

Details of your syllabus will be available to you somewhere. Normally, you will have a course handbook that tells you a lot of detail about exactly what you're going to be required to learn for each module of study unit you're taking. Such information is usually given out at the start of a course, or may be on web pages on an intranet, or even the Internet. There's a lot you can do to take charge of your syllabus, instead of being a passive recipient. The following suggestions will help.

1. **Remember that it is indeed *your* syllabus.** It's you who's going to have to learn it, not your lecturers – they've already done it (one hopes). So make sure you have all the details of what's on your agenda, and keep an eye as your course progresses on what's already been covered and what's still to come.

2. **Look really carefully at the 'intended learning outcomes'.** Most syllabus documents explain what students are required to learn in the form of such outcomes. They are often expressed as statements of what students will be expected to have become able to do at the end of a unit of study. This means *you*.

3. **Work out what you're expected to be able to do already.** Syllabus content rarely starts entirely from scratch. Quite often, there will be information such as 'prerequisite knowledge and skills', which spells out what it is assumed that students can already do when starting a module. Check that

you have indeed got such things under your belt, and, where there's a gap, make it your business to catch up on your own initiative.

4. **There need not be any unpleasant surprises in exams.** Colleges are required to link each and every element of assessment to the intended learning outcomes as expressed in the syllabus documentation. If you know that you can achieve all the things you're intended to be able to do, you should automatically be able to tackle any assessment question well.

5. **Use the syllabus to help you choose which books to buy or borrow.** Especially when buying books, it's important to be looking for ones which cover large parts of a syllabus rather than expensive books with only a few pages about a little part of the syllabus.

6. **Use the syllabus to know what's coming next.** Sometimes your lecturers will tell you about the overall shape of their particular parts of the syllabus, but it's even better if you take the responsibility for knowing where you've been in a subject, where you are now, and what's coming up. When you know what's coming up next, your subconscious mind gets working on it, and you're more receptive to it as it unfolds in your lectures.

7. **Brainstorm ahead.** Now and then, pick on a small bit of the syllabus that hasn't yet been covered in your classes, and jot down what you already know about this topic. Also jot down what you don't yet know about it, in the form of a list of questions to which you may need to find answers. You'll find that when you've done such a brainstorm, you're much more alert and receptive when your lecturers get round to teaching about such a topic, because you've already started thinking about it, and your mind is searching for the answers to some questions.

8. **Compare one subject's syllabus with that of the others.** This helps you to spot the links between the different subjects you're studying. This means that it's easier for you to get your head round the 'big picture' rather than just learning unconnected bits and pieces. In turn, you'll then be better able to give well-rounded answers to questions in exams and coursework assignments.

9. **Pick parts of the syllabus to cover under your own steam.** Your lecturers may well cover them in due course, but you'll be surprised how much better you understand them if you've already had a go at understanding them by yourself.

10. **Look ahead towards the end of each syllabus.** Exam questions will be set to cover the whole of any syllabus, but it's not unusual for teaching time to run out before everything has been taught.

11. **Cross-check between your syllabus and past exam papers.** There should be close links between the exam questions and the intended learning outcomes. Seeing the exam questions helps you to work out what the learning outcomes really mean in practice, and allows you to gauge the standards that are expected of you.

Part II

Lectures, Labs, Computers, Portfolios and so on

Don't Just *Take* Notes, *Make* Notes

The notes you make in lectures (and other learning situations) are among the most important of the resources you build up during your studies. However, many people just *take* notes, and this is not nearly as valuable as *making* notes. The suggestions below will help you to tell the difference, and then decide how to build *note making* into your overall study strategy. This set of tips is about lectures, where you're making notes under your own steam, without handout materials to write on. We'll then look at how to extend note making to handouts in the next set of tips.

1. **Take the view that you're only really learning if you're doing something with a pen or pencil.** Of course, if the lecture is just for entertainment, and you're not expected to remember anything from it, you don't need pen and paper! But most lectures *are* for learning from – at least that's what your lecturers are expecting. So use that pen to get your brain working, but don't just use it busily, use it *wisely*. Read on . . .

2. **Make your notes file-able.** One way of doing this is to put a little grid at the top of the first page, such as:

Monday	13		March
10–11	'The Impressionists: Monet'		Prof. Oakwood

3. **Don't just copy things down, even if everyone else is doing just that!** Don't just write down what you see on the screen or board, or word for word what the lecturer says. It's very easy to copy things down without even thinking about them. Copying things down is just note *taking* and may not even involve your brain!

4. **Put things into your own words.** This is note *making*, and necessarily involves you in thinking about what you're writing. Just sometimes you'll need to *take* notes, however (for example if you're expected to write down an exact definition or quotation). But for most of the time, what you should try to do is to capture for yourself the *essence* of what's being said and shown in lectures.

5. **Go *meaning-hunting*.** Don't write long sentences word for word. Instead, *summarize* what's being said or shown in a few well-chosen words of your own. Think about what is really *meant* by what you see and hear, and capture the meaning. This keeps you alert, and helps to stop you becoming bored, even when the topic (and/or the lecturer) seem quite boring!

6. **Take your own decision about when to write, and what to write.** Don't just write things down because everyone else is writing them down. Don't worry if you're the only one who is writing sometimes, others will probably soon be following your example. Make notes whenever you feel there's something worth capturing.

7. **Keep asking yourself: 'What am I expected to be able to do with this?'** This is one of the most important tips in this book! When you're asking this, you can deliberately and consciously make your notes so that they remind you of what seems to be expected of you. Keep adding to your notes little pointers (perhaps in a different colour) to alert you to what *you* may need to be able to show of what you've learned from the lecture.

8. **Go clue-detecting. What is really, really important?** Lecturers give all sorts away during a lecture by tone of voice, emphasis, body language and repetition. Sometimes they give these clues deliberately. Even more often, they do it subconsciously. Either way, *you* are the person who needs to

know what is really important, so that you can make sure you have a firm grip on such things.

9. **Make important things stand out in your notes.** Aim to make each page such that you can later tell at a glance what the main ideas or concepts are. Use colour, boxes, highlighters, patterns, and any other pet tricks you can think of to make the important stuff stand out on the page from the background stuff. Most of the marks in your assessments and exams will be linked to the important stuff. Deciding which is which can only be done well *during* the lecture, when you've got tone of voice, and so on to help you. It's much more difficult to go back to your notes weeks later and decide what's important.

10. **Write down your own questions.** Every time there's something you can't quite understand, turn it into a short question and write it down (maybe in a special colour just for such questions). When you've captured these questions, you can find out the answers in your own time, looking them up or asking other people, or asking the lecturer. If you hadn't written down your questions, a few hours later you wouldn't even remember what the questions were, and then there's no chance at all of getting them answered.

11. **Write down your own reactions, feelings and thoughts.** Quite often in a lecture you'll 'see the light dawn' about something, but if you didn't jot down something about that dawning, it might not happen again even when you read through your notes. Some people draw a lightbulb beside the idea that has just dawned for them, to remind them to make sure that the light can be switched on again at will later.

12. **Experiment with page layout.** Try to make every page of your notes look different. This helps every page to be more memorable. You'll sometimes find yourself at an exam desk weeks later thinking back to how a particular page of your notes *looks*, prompting your memory to something important from that page you now need to use.

13. **Compare *your* lecture notes with other people's.** Find two or three fellow-students who are really keen to turn their lecture notes into better notes by sharing and comparing.

You'll always find some useful things they wrote which you didn't. You can now add these into your notes. You can put right things you wrote down wrongly. The people you're sharing with can improve their notes by doing the same with yours. You all end up with a better set of notes, and will all do better in forthcoming assessments.

Making the Most of Handout Materials

You'll get loads of handout materials in most of your subject areas. Sometimes they'll be given out in lectures, and there will be yet more relating to other aspects of your studies such as practical work, field trips, seminars and so on. Sometimes, producing the handouts may be put into your court – for example, when lecturers make available text files or presentation files on an intranet. The following suggestions will help you to get high learning pay-off from your handouts.

1. **Make them *your* handouts.** For a start, put your name onto them, and the date you got them, and the topic or module concerned – this can save a lot of trouble later when trying to work out exactly where they fit in to your growing collection of paperwork.

2. **Don't copy down things that are already in your handouts.** Follow the tips in the previous section on *making* notes rather than *taking* notes. Add to your handouts, rather than duplicating things already in them. Use your time and energy making decisions about the material you're learning.

3. **Don't switch off just because you've got a handout.** This is particularly important when lecturers give you paper copies of the slides or overheads they use during lectures. Sometimes you'll get handouts covering three slides per page, with space for you to make notes alongside the slides. Sometimes you'll get six slides per page without extra space, and so on. It's dangerously easy to think, 'Ah well, I've got all the slides in

my handout, so I don't have to think hard about it now during the lecture – I can catch up later!'

4. **Use your handouts to capture important things.** During a lecture, there will be countless cues regarding what is really important. Use a highlighter pen to *show* such things in your handouts. Think about using two different colours of highlighter pen, for example one to indicate things you intend to look up or research further, and another to mark out things you know you need to remember.

5. **Write questions all over your handouts!** In various parts of this book, I've stressed the value of deciding what questions you need to become able to answer. During a lecture, when you can think of something you may well need to become able to do, jot it down as a question onto your handout material. It can be useful to reserve a particular colour for such questions, so that you can spot the questions easily later – and start practising to ensure that you'll remain able to answer them when needed.

6. **File your handouts systematically.** For example, it can be worth having a ring binder or lever-arch file for each subject, and keep this at home or in your study-bedroom. Carry around a further ring binder in which to store handouts you're going to receive. It can also be useful to have last week's handouts in this portable file, with separator cards to file them by subject. This allows you to catch up on last week's lecture handouts before or during this week's lecture and so on. Remove older materials to their separate home files from time to time as your portable binder becomes heavier.

7. **If you're using a ring binder, invest in a punch.** It can save you hours in the long run to have your handouts stored systematically. Loose piles of handout materials seem remarkably adept at rearranging themselves into random order! Therefore, punching and filing handouts regularly spares you from wasting valuable time looking for particular handout materials – for example the briefing sheet for an assignment due in next week, and so on.

8. **Turn intranet files and presentations into handouts.** When lecturers make available handout materials or presentations online through an intranet, it's usually

worthwhile getting them onto paper, and placing them in the right place alongside your other paper-based materials. Sometimes you may only be able to download and print such files *after* a lecture, in which case it's really useful to work your way right through them within a day or two of the lecture itself, turning them into your own materials by adding notes and questions as suggested above. If you can, of course, print off your copy of the materials *before* the lecture, and take the handout with you, and do your annotating *during* the lecture.

9. **If you miss a lecture, remember that the handout itself is no substitute for having been there.** Even in the most boring of lectures, there are things you could have done to the handout material, if you'd been there, which would have increased the learning pay-off associated with the handout. If you necessarily have to miss a lecture, but manage to get a copy of the handout which was issued there, try to catch up on what you might have gained if you'd been there. For example, try to look at the notes which two or three people who *were* there made, especially if they've marked up their copies of the handout along the lines suggested in the tips above.

10. **Don't just *read* handouts as you revise.** Turn them into lists of questions to practise answering – and concise summaries to help you reduce the content of your growing files of handouts to manageable proportions. Aim to make your summaries and question lists your *primary* study materials, so that you only have to go back to the more bulky original handouts from time to time to look up particular things when necessary.

Keeping on Top of Practical Work

In many subjects, practical work can be among the most enjoyable aspects of studying. It gives you the chance to link theory to practice, and even more important, it's usually fun. However, it's vital to keep a balance between practical work and all the other things you need to do, and the following tips will help you to adopt a sensible strategy.

1. **Don't go into practical work 'cold'.** Try to do some preparation for it – even just a few minutes can be really useful. Read through any printed instructions you've been issued in advance. Check up quickly on any background theory you may already be expected to have got to grips with.
2. **Work out the purpose of the practical work.** Seems obvious, but practical work is there for a reason, and it's worth keeping your eye on the intended learning outcomes that may be associated directly with it, showing you the targets to be gained from the work.
3. **Keep your jottings safe.** It's well worth making all of your notes in a rough book rather than on odd bits of paper – you're far less likely to lose a book than odd sheets. Even if handouts are issued for you to fill in as you do the practical work, have your own jottings safe in your own book as well.
4. **Don't forget to record the date, and the title of the practical activity.** This makes it so much easier, perhaps weeks later, to work out which of your jottings relate to which practical task, and avoid any possibility of getting mixed up

between one practical activity and another when writing up your respective reports.

5. **Capture your observations.** Write down in your rough book exactly what you see – even when you don't yet know what it might mean. Don't depend on your memory to recall details – save your memory for more important things, and jot down exactly what happens as your practical work proceeds.

6. **Find out exactly what sort of report or 'write-up' is expected.** Look at your course documentation for details relating to report writing. More importantly, find out from your tutors about what they are really looking for in practical reports. For example, sometimes you may be asked to write 'full' reports, and other times 'short-form' or 'memorandum' reports.

7. **Adopt a 'same day' approach.** When possible, aim to write up your practical work within 24 hours of doing the work, at least in a full draft version. This saves you hours and hours, as it's far quicker to write your reports when you can remember exactly what you did, and when all the jottings in your own rough book still make perfect sense to you.

8. **Finish off the 'central' parts of your report first.** These normally include report sections such as 'method' or 'procedure', 'observations', 'data', 'analysis of data', and so on. These are the parts which you really need to get onto paper (or disk) as soon as possible, while the work is fresh in your memory.

9. **Pay particular attention to the interpretation of your findings.** Most of the marks are likely to be for interpretation of your results, not just your results themselves.

10. **Come to clear conclusions.** Most practical work needs to lead to one or more definite conclusions, and your conclusions need to be clearly visible in your report (usually near the end, but before any appendices), so that you have the maximum chance of gaining marks for coming clearly to conclusions.

11. **Be particularly meticulous about error limits.** You'll probably have had some training in how to estimate the effects of sources of experimental error, and how to carry

through into your analysis the statistical effects of such error sources on your conclusions.

12. **Compare your findings with published data.** Whenever possible, note in your report the agreement (or indeed the *disagreement*) between your findings and other published data, taking great care to include the references to published findings carefully and accurately in your report.

13. **Avoid backlogs of practical reports at all costs!** If you get into the position of having such a backlog, one piece of practical work begins to merge with another, and it gets far harder to write sensible reports. More importantly, however, the last thing you need when it is time to prepare for vital exams is a backlog of practical reports to deal with!

14. **Hand in your practical reports on time – or earlier.** Tutors often notice that reports handed in punctually tend to be rather better than those that come in late.

15. **Don't be a perfectionist.** Hand in your reports even if you're still not entirely satisfied with them. Even a mediocre report, handed in on time, is likely to score around half-marks. A perfect report that is *not* handed in at all scores exactly zero marks!

Using Print-based Open Learning Materials

Many courses use open learning materials for at least *some* of the provision they include. It is indeed possible to have entire courses in open learning mode – the Open University in the UK, for example, runs whole degrees and postgraduate programmes by open learning. The following tips should help you to tune in your own ways of studying to make the most of such learning formats.

1. **Sort out the various jargon terms for yourself.** 'Open learning' is about learning not done in lectures or tutorials or seminars, and is usually based around issued learning materials – print-based or computer-based. In open learning you have at least some freedom about when, where and how fast you study. You may even have some freedom about *what* you study. 'Flexible learning' is another term given to this sort of studying. Sometimes it's called 'distance learning' (for example as used by the Open University in the UK – students don't all go to its Milton Keynes base to study!). If you're away from college on work placement, you may well be doing some 'distance learning' as well while you're there. There are yet more possible terms, including 'self-study pathways' and 'independent learning module', and so on. All of these are about a focus on the learning, and not the teaching.

2. **Find out the scale of your open learning.** For example, find out how much it counts for. Is it the same number of credit points as a 'taught' unit? Is there any indication to tell

you approximately how many hours it is supposed to take you? When will you fit these hours into your busy life? – not all just before the exams! Will it be assessed in the same exams as other parts of your course? How long have you got? Will there be tutor-marked assignments at particular stages through the open learning work?

3. **Sort out what you're assumed to be able to do already.** Most open learning packages give some information about the 'prerequisites' – knowledge or skills you are expected to have already gained. If you're already up to scratch on these things, you can get started straight away on your open learning. If not, however, it could be well worth tackling the shortfall, and finding some books or courses which will help you catch up on what you will need to bring to your particular open learning element of study.

4. **Look for the objectives, or intended learning outcomes.** Any well-designed open learning package will state these quite clearly. These tell you what it's going to be about – but, more importantly, they give you information about the standards you're expected to achieve as a result of your learning. They're often expressed with wording such as, 'When you've worked through this package, you should be able to . . .', followed by a list of the things you'll be able to *show* for your learning.

5. **Open learning materials focus on 'learning by doing'.** The best such materials are full of things for you to do as you work through them. The activities may have all sorts of names – exercises, quizzes, self-assessment questions, and so on, but the important thing is to *do* them and not just to *read* them.

6. **Well-designed open learning materials don't *just* ask you to do things.** They give you feedback on what you've done. For example, if there are self-assessment questions for you to have a go at, there will also be *feedback responses* for you to look at after you've made your own attempt. These allow you to compare what you did with what you *should* have done.

7. **Remember that you're not expected to learn everything in the package!** Most open learning materials contain a great deal of information. You're only expected to turn *some* of this into your own knowledge. Some of it is just explanation,

background, perspective-setting material and so on. The clues pointing you towards exactly *which parts* you need to concentrate on have already been mentioned above – the learning outcomes and the activities in the materials.

8. **When you come to an activity – do it!** Don't just skip it and turn to the response to see what the right answer might have been. That way you'll have learned very little. Have a go at each activity, *resisting* any temptation to look ahead to the feedback response to find out whether you're on the right lines. You'll learn far more by having a *real* go at the activity, *then* finding out whether you were right or not.

9. **When you find you've got something right – be pleased.** Remind yourself of *what* you got right. You may need this particular bit of knowledge for a later assignment or exam. Don't just let it slip away again. Make sure that you can still get it right tomorrow and the next day – especially if you have already twigged that it's really important.

10. **When you find that you got something wrong – be even more pleased!** Look at the feedback response and find out exactly *what* you got wrong. Work out *why* you got it wrong. This is one thing less for you to get wrong next time – or in an assignment, or in an exam. Check that you will now be able to do whatever it was correctly. Check next day that you can *still* do it correctly, and so on.

11. **Make the most of learning in the comfort of privacy.** With open learning materials, no one but you knows when you've messed up an activity. So you can learn from your mistakes without any embarrassment. This is one of the advantages of open learning over class-based activities.

12. **Keep looking back.** One danger with open learning packages is that of just pressing ever onwards, without going back and reminding yourself of what you've covered. The knowledge you gain by doing the activities and comparing your efforts with the feedback responses will only *stay* with you if you keep it topped up. It doesn't take long to scan through what you've already covered now and then to *refresh* your knowledge – and is well worth the time it takes.

13. **Keep looking forward too.** With print-based packages (unlike some computer-based ones), you can flick ahead easily

to see what's coming next, and where that leads, and so on. Seeing what's coming next often helps you to see *why* you're doing something now, and if you know *why* you're doing something, it's easier to concentrate on it. It's useful to have your eye on the 'big picture' so that you always know where the little bit you're presently working on fits in. It's a bit like a jigsaw – you may only handle one piece at a time, but you can't do much with it without looking at where it belongs.

14. **Make the most of your freedom about *when* you learn.** With open learning materials, you can learn from them any time you choose. Choose to use them when a bit of open learning will be a nice change from (for example) writing that essay or finishing off that practical write-up.

15. **Enjoy the freedom of *where* you learn.** You can use print-based open learning materials just about anywhere you can have the materials with you – at home, on trains, on beaches, you name it. Choose to do at least some of your open learning in places you can regard as relaxation areas too. You can't so easily use freedom of place with computer-based materials, so make the most of such freedom where you can.

16. **If the materials *belong* to you, make them your own.** Write on them. Answer questions in them. Put down *your* questions in them. Put down your passing thoughts in them. Then later when you look back at them, you will quickly catch up with your own thinking – better than wasting it. Obviously, if you've just been *loaned* the print-based packages, you can't make them your own in these ways.

17. **Look ahead every now and then to how your learning is going to be measured.** Look at old exam questions if your open learning is to be tested in an exam. Get your hands on tutor-marked assignment questions if it's going to be continuously assessed. Or both. Find out more about *which* parts of the content of the open learning package lend themselves to being assessed. There may indeed be interesting parts of the package that have no connections with assessment at all. If so the message is clear – don't spend too much time on these parts.

Keeping on Top of Your Emails

You may well be very familiar with email, and use it all the time to keep in touch with friends. Most institutions also use email as one of the communications channels between tutors and students, and it could even be an important part of your course. The following tips will help you to make the most of email communication with tutors, fellow-students and anyone else.

1. **Check your emails often.** If you don't, you could miss out on important things, such as briefing notes from tutors about assignments, changes to timetabled sessions, and feedback on marked work (not to mention social arrangements with friends, and all the rest).

2. **Build up your 'address book'.** Some systems allow this to happen automatically, storing the details of everyone you send to. Usually, however, it's up to you to add to your address book the details of people you receive from – such as, for example, your tutors. Normally, all you have to do is double-click the 'from' details at the top of an incoming email for a prompt to add the address to your own electronic address book.

3. **Don't lose your address book!** From time to time, print it out (if you can), or save it as a file on floppy disk and transfer it to your own machine. It's not always easy to move address books between one system and another, so a back-up system for retaining old-but-important addresses can save you sweat.

4. **Find out when best to get onto a machine.** At busy times, you can waste a lot of time queuing for a place at a terminal, and wasting time on anything is not part of your success strategy! At other times, the machines may be much quieter. If you find yourself queuing, try to have things with you to do as you queue, such as polishing up your 'top ten points about topic X' which you've conveniently captured on a sheet of paper or filing card for just such occasions.

5. **Watch your language.** Email is an informal communications medium, to say the least. It's important to adjust your tone and style of language appropriately when emailing tutors – some of whom are likely to be offended if you're too laid back in your tone. Also, most institutions have quite strict codes about sending anything offensive by electronic means, and sometimes expel people for putting anything really offensive through their systems.

6. **Don't accumulate a gigantic 'inbox'.** It becomes impossible to track down something important from weeks ago when there are thousands of emails in your inbox. Most email systems allow you to create folders and sub-folders, and it's well worth organising your incoming emails into a sensible filing system, so that you can quickly track down anything important that you need to revisit. If you use email on several different courses or modules, it's worth creating separate folders for these, as well as for the different people you often contact by email.

7. **Don't accumulate a huge 'sent' box.** Once you've created folders for people and modules, it's well worth the time spent to now and then file your 'sent' messages in the appropriate folders, so that you can find out quickly what *you* said in reply to what they said, and so on.

8. **Don't run out of space on the server.** You'll probably have limited space on your institution's server. If your space gets full, it usually means that incoming messages will be bounced back and won't reach you. You may not even be aware that this is happening, and may only find out when *you* try to email someone.

9. **Try to back up important things.** These include assignment briefings, timetable-change information, and so

on. You may be able to download these to floppy disk, or transfer them to your own machine, or print them out. It's well worth avoiding the situation of being desperate to find details that are only available in an email on an institution's server which has gone down!

10. **Choose your message title carefully.** If you don't give your email a title, there's a chance it won't even be read. It's best if your title looks interesting enough to tempt your reader to open the email. It's also helpful if the title indicates quite clearly what the email is about. If you're replying to an email, the original title will normally be reproduced, with 're . . .' added, which is useful. However, don't allow titles to become longer than three or four words, otherwise readers are likely to see only the first few words of the title on-screen.

11. **Keep your emails short.** Most people only look at what comes up on the screen first, so convey the gist of your message in the first few lines. If you intend your reader to download or print out the message, say so at this point.

12. **Send attachments for longer things.** If you're sending long documents (spreadsheets, pictures, and so on), while it is sometimes possible to paste them directly into an email, it's usually much better to send them as attached files. Send yourself a copy, so that you can check for yourself that the attached files were indeed attached. If you include in your message words along the lines of 'please see attached file. . . .', it's a good idea to attach the file *immediately* after you type the word 'attach', otherwise you'll forget to attach it (like I do!).

Computer Conferencing

In some discipline areas, you could get the chance to join computer conferences. A variety of formats exist, ranging from quite sophisticated ones (for example using 'Blackboard' software) to simple email discussion lists. If electronic communication possibilities of this kind come your way, the following suggestions may help you make the most of them.

1. **Don't be a lurker!** Join in. The term 'lurker' is applied to people who just watch what's going on in a computer conference or email discussion list, but who don't actually take part. Some software systems can actually display who's logged in to a conference at any given time, so it could be noticed that you're just lurking there.

2. **Keep your contributions short and focused.** It's well known that most people only read the first line or two of an email or computer-conference contribution, unless they are really interested. Therefore make sure that your first couple of lines are really interesting and relevant, if you want people to read what else you have to say.

3. **Check whether your participation is assessed.** Sometimes, an email discussion list or computer conference may be an assessed part of your coursework. When this is the case, one of the simplest things that can be done is simply to count the number of contributions you've made over a given time.

4. **Don't 'flame' people.** This is the term given to disagreeing

strongly with someone else's contribution to the conference or discussion list, and expressing your disagreement in a way which could be taken to be insulting or derogatory. Apart from the risk of offending the originator of the contribution you're criticizing, don't forget that if your tone or style is offensive, everyone else participating sees it too.

5. **Find out whether the system allows you to 'recall' an email.** This is sometimes possible, and can be useful if you have second thoughts about a contribution after you've sent it. However, most systems don't allow such luxuries, so as a rule it's much safer to make sure that you're entirely satisfied with a contribution *before* you send it. Some systems allow you to 'save drafts' in a separate folder, and return to them later before you send them.

6. **Ask questions.** One of the most useful ways to be active in a discussion list is to be one of the people who asks questions, rather than just responding to others' ideas. But try to make sure that your questions are quite short, sharp and straightforward. The problem with complex questions is that no one gets round to working out what they really mean, and they don't generate nearly so much discussion as would two or three equivalent short questions.

7. **Find out about printing.** Sometimes there may be a printer beside the computer or terminal. Alternatively, there may be a printer somewhere else entirely – perhaps in a different room or building. Sometimes you may have to pay for your printing. It's useful to check such things out, so you can decide whether and when to print out particular items from the discussion for future reference.

8. **Find out how to save contributions.** You may be able to save and download useful contributions to your own floppy disk, and install them on your own computer. It's useful to check this out first, as your computer may not already have the software to read downloaded files. If you save contributions regularly, you will need to find a good way of organizing those you save – the titles and dates may not be enough for you to recall which contribution contained the pearl of wisdom for which you saved it.

9. **Find out how to start new topics.** It is very easy to reply to

existing messages in a conference, but it is sometimes worth starting a new 'thread' or topic. When you do this, you'll need to think of a title for the 'thread'. Make the title short. If you make it too long, it will probably not all be readable on-screen, particularly if it is in an indented list. Also make it as self-explanatory as possible, so that people choosing to open your contribution know what to expect.

10. **Decide when best to start new topics.** New threads often arise out of existing threads in the discussion. The problem is that if they just stay there, it is not obvious that a new theme has emerged. Therefore, it's sometimes worth including in your reply 'I'm now starting a new thread called [whatever it is] to follow up this idea . . .'.

Getting to Know Your Word Processor

If you've got your own computer, you'll doubtless have played with word-processing software already. If not, you're likely to meet such software during your course. You may in fact be *required* to submit at least some coursework assignments in word-processed format – or even electronically via email. The following suggestions should encourage you to make the most of your opportunities to learn how to produce good documents.

1. **Don't be scared of breaking it!** Like anything else to do with computers, it's *extremely* unlikely that you'll break it (provided you don't get so frustrated with it that you drop it from a great height!).

2. **What's in it for you?** Being able to type well and use a word processor is in your own interests. It all saves you time when you're applying for jobs, updating your CV, and communicating via email. You're also likely to be regarded as being that bit more employable if these skills are in your portfolio. Gone are the days when everyone had a secretary to do their paperwork for them – even Chief Executives are quite likely to do at least some of their own typing nowadays (especially, of course, the confidential documents).

3. **What's the *worst* thing that's likely to happen to you?** It happens to everyone sooner or later, but usually only *once*! One day you'll have been working away for a couple of hours at a document, so engrossed that you don't bother to save it along the way, and the machine will freeze up, or there'll be a

power cut, or someone will trip over a cable and disconnect your machine, and so on. In short, your work will be lost. It could be recoverable, but usually isn't. You'll simply have to start all over again. We've all done this – but only once. Henceforth, you'll save your work every few minutes.

4. **But don't just save and save and save.** Use the 'Save as . . .' command instead. The file I'm writing at this moment (and you're reading now) is called 'wordprocessor tips 1'. A few minutes later I'll save it as 'wordprocessor tips 2' and so on. By the time I get to 'wordprocessor tips 14' it might be time to call the next version 'wordprocessor tips final'. The advantage of saving your file under a *different* name each time is that you can, when necessary, go back to *earlier* versions. If, for example, you delete a whole paragraph from your essay, and then on second thoughts wish to include it again, you can only do this if you can still get back to an earlier version. If you just had been using the 'save' command all the time, you'd have *replaced* each earlier version with its successor.

5. **Keep records of your filenames.** If you're doing a lot of word processing, the most common problem is forgetting what you called the document you were working on last week. You may be able to find it by searching your files in *date* order, but that's not as good as making your filename titles quite self-explanatory.

6. **Don't be frightened at how much your word processor can do.** Few people, if any, use *all* of the features on a modern word-processing package. Most use just a tiny fraction of the features. For most purposes – including producing essays or reports – you'll only actually need the most basic features. So don't look through all the menus thinking 'What on earth am I going to do with *this*?'

7. **Develop your keyboard skills.** If you've got time and energy to turn yourself into a touch typist, using all of your fingers, it will save you time in the long run. If, for example, you're going on towards a dissertation, and then a doctoral thesis, and journal articles, books and fame, being able to type fast and accurately saves a lot of time and energy. There are many typing-tutor software programs that can help you to teach yourself to type properly. There may also be face-to-face

courses at a local college. One of the advantages of touch typing is speed – you could easily become able to type a lot faster than you can write – and without your fingers getting tired so quickly.

8. **Learn typing by doing typing.** Even if you're not going in for the full touch-typing business, you'll speed up if you use your computer for word processing whenever it's sensible to do so. You could use it for your shopping lists, letters to friends, emails, essay drafts, summary notes, question-bank components, and all sorts of things, before you get round to using it for assessed coursework.

9. **Always be prepared to ask.** With a word-processing package, it's often far quicker to get someone who knows to instruct you on how to do something you've been trying to do. You can, of course, find out how to do things using the manual that accompanies the software, or the various 'help' menus built in to the package, but help from someone who knows *how* to do what *you* want to do is often a lot faster.

10. **Become your own editor.** Develop your skills at editing on-screen. The really useful features are 'copy', 'cut', and 'paste'. You can use your mouse to select a word or sentence, and then move it up or down into another place in your document. This is far easier and faster than having to *write* out a whole paragraph again for such a change.

11. **Print things out now and then to see how they look.** *Some* editing you can do on-screen, but there will be times when you need to see how your whole page looks before you can make adjustments.

12. **Keep a printed back-up copy of anything important.** If the worst happens – your machine breaks or is stolen, your only disk corrupts, and so on – all is not lost if you've at least got a paper version of the work you've done so far. You may indeed have to type it all out again in such circumstances, but at least you haven't got all that *thinking* to do again. And, in practice, you may be able to get it *scanned* back into a computer file from your printed copy, using a machine with some OCR (optical character recognition) software.

13. **Consider including the filename in a header or footer on your draft document.** This means that every time you

print out a section of what you're writing, each page will tell you which draft it was. You can include the date too, if that helps. When later you want to know *which* draft was the particular piece of paper you're holding, you will then have no problem.

14. **Don't worry about spelling too much.** In your *final* version of an essay or report, you'll need to have got your spelling right, and the spell-check facilities on your word processor can help you greatly. But in intermediate drafts, it's often better to simply ignore spelling, and therefore to type faster, without going back to correct every mistake.

15. **Worry more about grammar!** Although most word processors have 'grammar-checking' software as well as 'spell-checks', the former is rarely much use in practice. A grammar check may tell you that a particular sentence is too long, but not much more than that. At the end of the day, it's *you* who will need to sort out your grammar and punctuation, so you might as well keep an eye on these things continuously as you use your word processor.

16. **Develop your eye for layout.** Don't just fill every page from top to bottom. Look for ways of making your page look *interesting*, for example by using headings and subheadings, a line of space between paragraphs, and so on. Experiment with the different print fonts at your disposal, but don't use several of these on the same page – that annoys people, including those who may be going to assess your final work.

17. **Experiment with the different styles you can use.** For example, even the most basic word-processors can print **bold**, *italic*, ***bold italic***, <u>underlined</u>, **<u>bold-underlined</u>**, and so on. In some fonts these different styles look better than others. But don't over-use such powerful formats as bold-underlined. Nor put too much in upper-case, CAPITALS. While the odd word is fine in capitals, a whole sentence looks intimidating, and is known as 'shouting' in email (or web-design) 'netiquette'.

18. **Consider going on a word-processing course.** Most institutions provide these, often run by Computing Services Departments or suchlike. It could cost you nothing except a few hours of your time. You may need to book well in ‚ advance. But the *best* time to go on this sort of course is when

you're already *using* your word processor quite a lot, so that you *know* which tricks are going to be really useful to you when you meet them in the course. Like most things, if you go on a course *before* you get round to putting it into practice, you'll then find you've forgotten most of the things that seemed perfectly straightforward while you were doing the course.

Making IT Training Work for You

Most institutions provide a wide range of training courses relating to computers, communications technologies, email, the Internet and various aspects of modern technology. Your own course may well include such elements. Whether or not this is the case, there's a lot you can do to get good value from such provision. The following tips may encourage you to make the most of the opportunities around you.

1. **Don't rest on your laurels.** You may well be very comfortable with computers, email, the Internet and so on. You may indeed be better at using these things than some of your lecturers are. But the world of information and communications technologies continues to move fast, and you don't want it to move right past you while you're concentrating on being a successful student.
2. **Find out what's on offer, and when, and where.** The 'Information Services' (or whatever your institution calls it) section may well provide a programme of short courses, open to students. Library staff will be able to tell you more, and may indeed be involved in running such courses themselves. There are likely to be posters on notice-boards, and flyers lying around the place. Somewhere in your institution's provision will be training on word processors, PowerPoint, databases, designing web pages, and all sorts of things specific to particular software packages.
3. **Don't just think about what's relevant to you at the**

moment. For example, you might not have any immediate need to find out about how to make a database, but some day this could be really useful for you. In any case, learning is never wasted. New software comes out all the time, and the more software you've got your head round, the quicker you become at learning to use new software.

4. **Check that you can take part.** In some institutions, you may need, as a student, authorization from someone in your own department to apply for a place. In addition, you may need to check whether there are any conflicts between the date and time of the training course and your own study programme – particularly assessment timetables.

5. **Remind yourself that such courses are usually free of charge.** Exactly the same training programmes may cost an arm and a leg in commerce or industry. You have, in effect, got the opportunity to get some really useful training for nothing except the time you put into it. Later when you set about job hunting, you can include details of the training you will have had as a valuable asset in your curriculum vitae.

6. **Book early.** Many of the most popular courses fill up rapidly. Since such training ties up roomfuls of computers, the number of places is limited. And whatever you do, don't not turn up! When provision is in high demand, a dim view is taken of anyone who's booked a valuable place and then fails to appear on the day.

7. **Get there on time.** Short courses depend on people being punctual, and it's important not to miss the beginning, when handout materials may be issued, and other vital information supplied.

8. **Regard it as recreation.** If you're doing something completely different for a day, it can be a useful break from your regular studies. Don't just let it all wash over you, however – give it your best shot. The more you put in, the more you'll get out of it.

9. **Don't be afraid to ask for help.** Normally there will be a wide range of experience among the course participants. Some will need hardly any help, while others will be struggling. Ask for help from people sitting close to you when necessary. Help them too when you can – there's nothing

better than showing someone else how to do something with a computer for helping you to remember really well how to do it yourself.

10. **Don't be too critical of the teaching.** Sometimes there will be the usual kind of questionnaire to fill in about your experience of the training course. Perhaps you've encountered far better teachers elsewhere in your studies, but the important thing is to get what you can out of the course, not to try too much to change the course. Sometimes the people running the training courses will be experts in the software, but not highly trained in teaching. (That also applies, of course, to some of your regular lecturers!)

11. **'But what if there's nothing suitable available to me?'** It can be worth looking around for alternatives. There may be a local college not far away which offers a programme of short evening courses. You may indeed have to pay for these, but they're not usually for millionaires only.

12. **Don't let it all slip away from you again.** While you're sitting there at your computer in the course venue, you're likely to be on a rapid learning curve, and gaining all sorts of skills with the software you're using. Only a week or two later, you could have forgotten key steps, and find it really hard to get back into it. The ideal approach is to find yourself an opportunity to practise again using what you've learned. Check out which machines or terminals are available to you to practise on. If necessary, book yourself some time slots when you can do this.

13. **Try to do something with what you've learned.** For example, if you've been on a word-processor course, practise by turning some of your written notes into useful summaries. If you've been on a PowerPoint course, start practising making presentations, so that when you need to do this for real you will be able to do so much more efficiently.

Getting Your Reflections onto Paper

It's always useful to think about how your learning is going – we called it 'making sense of things' or 'digesting' earlier in this book. You could be *required* to 'reflect' on your learning. You may be asked to write a 'reflective log' as part of a portfolio alongside your studies. 'What *is* reflection in such contexts? And *how* can I reflect? How will I know when I've reflected well?' are questions which students ask about the process. Moreover, 'How can I *show* that I've reflected successfully? What will be deemed satisfactory *evidence* of my reflection?' are their next questions. The short answer to many of these questions is that reflection can best be captured by asking yourself questions, and then working out your answers to those questions and writing them down in a suitable way. Just about all the best questions have the letter 'w' in the key interrogative word – who, what, when, where, why and how, for example.

1. **Why is it useful for you to reflect?** Reflection deepens your learning. The act of reflecting is one which causes us to make sense of what we've learned, why we learned it, and how that particular increment of learning took place. Reflection is equally useful when our learning has been unsuccessful – in such cases indeed reflection can often give us insights into what may have gone wrong with our learning, and how on a future occasion we might avoid now-known pitfalls.
2. **Reflection is a useful transferable skill.** It is much valued by employers. If your course involves you putting together a portfolio, this could be of considerable interest to future

employers, who will be able to find out a lot more about you than they could have learned just from your exam results or the qualifications you've achieved.

3. **Why write your reflections down?** Have *you* reflected today? Almost certainly, 'Yes!' But have you *evidenced* your reflection today? Almost certainly, 'Sorry, too busy at the moment.' And the danger remains that even the best of reflection is volatile – it evaporates away unless we stop in our tracks to make one or other kind of crystallization of it – some evidence.

4. **Where, when and how might you need to capture your reflections?** *Evidence* of your reflection could be needed if, for example, you are required to build up 'personal development planning' portfolios, or learning logs, or records of achievement, both as evidence to be able to present to prospective employers, and (more importantly) as a proactive process to help you to deepen your ongoing learning as it happens.

5. **Reflection is best when past, present and future are being thought about.** For example, the following trio of questions is a lot more productive in generating reflection than any one of them would have been on its own:

   - What worked really well for you?
   - Why do you now think this worked well for you?
   - What are you going to do next as a result of this having worked well for you?

6. **There are all sorts of questions you can use to get your reflections going.** The remainder of this set of tips should be regarded as a provisional agenda for reflection. You've not got time to think about *all* of these questions. You will almost certainly come up with *better* questions of your own. But the best way to get into just what reflection is about is to see a range of possible questions, and work outward from there. Here are some questions, in little clusters, in no particular order, as food for thought – tick those which seem relevant to your own particular needs.

Questions to get your reflection going

Let's suppose you're reflecting on a piece of work you've just done, for example a coursework assignment. Here are some questions to get you thinking – and capturing your thoughts.

- What did I actually achieve with this piece of work? Which were the most difficult parts, and why were they difficult for me? Which were the most straightforward parts, and why did I find these easy?
- How well do I think I achieved the intended learning outcomes for this task? Where could I have improved my achievement? Why didn't I improve it at the time?
- What have I got out of doing this assignment? How have I developed my knowledge and skills? How do I see the pay-off from doing this assignment helping me in the longer term?
- What *else* have I got out of doing this assignment? Have I

developed other skills and knowledge, which may be useful elsewhere at another time? If so, what are my own *emergent* learning outcomes from doing this assignment?

- What was the best thing I did? Why was this the best thing I did? How do I know that this was the best thing I did?

- What worked least well for me? Why did this not work well for me? What have I learned about the topic concerned from this not having worked well for me? What have I learned about myself from this not having worked well for me? What do I plan to do differently in future as a result of my answers to the above questions?

- With hindsight, how would I go about this assignment differently if doing it again from scratch? To what extent will this assignment influence the way I tackle anything similar in future?

- What did I find the greatest challenge in doing this work? Why was this a challenge to me? To what extent do I feel I have met this challenge? What can I do to improve my performance when next meeting this particular sort of challenge?

- What was the most boring or tedious part of doing this assignment for me? Can I see the point of doing these things? If not, how could the assignment have been redesigned to be more stimulating and interesting for me?

- Has it been worth the effort I put in? Do the marks represent a just reward? Should this assignment be worth more or less marks in the overall scheme of things?

- Do I feel that my time on this assignment has been well spent? If not, how could I have used my time more sensibly? Or should the assignment have been designed differently? Which parts of the assignment represent the time best spent? Which parts could be thought of as time wasted?

- How useful do I expect the feedback on this assignment to be? What sorts of feedback do I really want at this point in time? What sorts of feedback do I really *need* at this point in time? What are my expectations of getting useful feedback now, based on the feedback (or lack of it) that I've already received on past work?

- Overall, how has this assignment helped (or hindered) my motivation to learn more about this part of my syllabus? Has it encouraged me, or disillusioned me?

- To what extent has this assignment helped me to clarify what I still need to learn about this topic? Have I a clearer picture after doing the assignment, or a foggier one? Who can help me gain a clearer picture, if the latter?

- To what extent has this assignment helped me to see where the goalposts stand for future assessments such as exams? Has it given me useful insights into what will be expected of me in future?
- What advice would I give to a friend about to start on the same assignment? How much time would I suggest that it would be worth putting into it? What pitfalls would I advise to be well worth not falling into?
- What are the three most important things that I think I need to do with this topic at this moment in time? Which of these do I think is the most urgent for me to do? When will I aim to start doing this, and what is a sensible deadline for me to have completed it by?

Building Your Portfolio

This may or may not be something that you'll have to do as part of your course. If it isn't, you can of course skip these tips. But even then, you may find in your later career that you will be expected to build or maintain a portfolio of your work or achievements, so come back to these tips then. If, however, a portfolio is on your immediate agenda, you may need help on how best to go about making one – it could well be something you haven't done before.

1. **Remind yourself *why* you want to build a portfolio.** It is best that you *want* to build one, rather than simply that you are required to build one for your course. It could turn out to be a useful piece of evidence to show prospective employers in the future. A good portfolio will tell people a lot more about you than simply your final exam results – however good they are.

2. **Check carefully the specific format suggested for your portfolio.** It helps to keep it firmly in mind both when collecting evidence and when annotating it with your own reflective commentaries. The previous set of tips should help you to decide how best to make such commentaries.

3. **Keep the assessment framework in sight.** While you can usually put anything *else* that you think is relevant into your portfolio if you want to, you will *need* to include evidence that relates directly to the assessment framework whereby your portfolio will be judged.

4. **Start collecting evidence straight away.** Much of the content of your portfolio will come from your day-to-day studying, or your ongoing work on a research project or work placement, and so on. The most efficient way of starting off a portfolio is to decide what sorts of evidence will be useful to you, and start collecting examples of this evidence as a normal part of your everyday work.

5. **Decide what sorts of evidence you will need.** The exact nature of your own evidence will depend upon the kind of portfolio you are building, and what the timescale is, and what the specification requires you to include.

6. **File your evidence systematically.** Don't just put it all in a file or a drawer! Sort it first, according to the particular sections of your portfolio that the evidence will go into. It is worth starting up a number of parallel files, to ensure you make it easy to decide where each element of your evidence should be stored.

7. **Decide on the physical form of your portfolio.** For example, you may decide to use a ring binder for the 'primary' evidence (your principal reflections, and other important evidence) and lever-arch file for your appendices ('secondary' evidence, examples of all sorts of other things which give further detail of what you've done, and so on). Such formats make it much easier to adjust the contents of your portfolio, or to rearrange the order in which you present sections.

8. **Don't use plastic wallets for things that need to be easy to read (and to assess!).** While it's fine to use such wallets to keep together sets of similar papers in appendices, it is very frustrating for a reader (or assessor) to have to take out individual primary evidence sheets to read them.

9. **Make a draft contents list.** Decide in which order you wish to present your main evidence. There is sometimes no 'right' order for headings and subheadings, even when the overall structure of the sections of the portfolio is laid down. The order of your headings and subheadings will depend on the nature of your work, and the range of evidence you wish to present. It is, however, very useful to have this order sorted out in your mind before you start to put together the 'front

end' of your portfolio, in other words, your reflections and commentaries about your evidence.

10. **Think of your target audience.** Who is going to read your portfolio? More importantly, who will perhaps make judgements on it? A really good portfolio will be *interesting* for them to browse through, *easy* for them to find their way backwards and forwards, and *non-repetitive* – won't have too many examples of the same kinds of evidence.

11. **Don't write the introduction yet!** The introduction to a portfolio is extremely important. As with essays, reports, and other assessment formats, there is no second chance to make a good first impression! You can only write a really good introduction when you know exactly what you're introducing, so leave the introduction till you've more or less finished everything else in your portfolio. You can, of course, write a *draft* introduction to pave the way for the better one you'll write later, but this is probably best done as a bullet-point list or as a mind-map sketch (for example, an 'egg diagram' as discussed elsewhere in this book).

12. **If your portfolio is going to be assessed, get other people to assess it against the assessment framework.** You could use fellow-students, or anyone else you can get to do this for you. You could even consider using their assessments of your portfolio as part of the evidence in your portfolio. When they find something missing, or suggest some further developments, you can annotate the assessment pro forma to show what you have done about it.

13. **Get other people's general feedback.** Another pair of eyes is always useful. Show draft bits of your portfolio to anyone you can who's likely to be interested. Ask them to scribble liberally over anything where it could be worth you having second thoughts, or further explanations. Ask them also not to hesitate in pointing out typographical or grammatical errors: it is always easier for someone else to find them than for us to spot our own!

14. **Self-assess your portfolio.** Use the marking scheme for the portfolio – if there is one and it is available to you – to find out how *you* think your portfolio lives up to what is expected. You may wish to include your self-assessment in

its own right as a further element of evidence in your portfolio.

15. **Now write the introduction.** It also helps enormously to present at the start a good contents page for both the primary evidence and the appendices, based on the draft contents list you started out with. Try to make sure that your portfolio is easy for any reader to navigate.

Part III

Essays

Planning that Essay

Elsewhere in this book we've looked at ways round the problem of getting started on tasks in general, but essays are special – there are even more ways of not getting round to doing them! Therefore, my tips on writing essays begin with the things you need to do before even starting on writing the essay itself.

1. **Get planning straight away.** As soon as you've got the title, there's absolutely nothing to stop you deciding to make your own gentle start. All the better if you know that the submission date seems years away – thinking without pressure can be much more creative than when your mind is full of anxiety, for example when the deadline is tomorrow.

2. **Starting your planning early means you've got much more scope to make it really good.** In other words, you've got plenty of time for revision, second thoughts, and further researching if your first rough draft is done really early. Also, there will be things you don't really understand at all this week, but where next week will bring the dawning of the light.

3. **Make the most of your brief.** Sometimes, you'll just have a title. But you may also have a breakdown of how many marks are going to go to each specific part of your essay – for example the beginning (stating or clarifying the question to be addressed or the case to be made), the middle, and the

end (coming to a decision, verdict, conclusion and so on).
This can be really useful guidance regarding how you spread
your efforts over the essay.

4. **Make good use of the related 'intended learning
   outcomes'.** Just about all assessed tasks are *meant* to relate in
   one way or another to one or more of the intended learning
   outcomes associated with your course or module. Sometimes
   the links are plain to see – such outcomes may be directly
   stated along with the essay briefing or instructions. At other
   times, you need to make your own links.

5. **Find out everything you can about how the essay will be
   marked in due course.** For example, in your course
   documentation you may well have grids of 'grade descriptors'.
   These may tell you really useful information about what makes
   the difference between a really good essay, an 'ordinary' one,
   and a fail! Find out all you can about what is being looked for
   in a good one, and steer your thinking and planning to meet
   this head on.

6. **Don't start at the beginning.** Tempting as it sometimes is to
   write the introduction straight away, that's the last thing you
   should do. Putting it the other way, the best thing to save to
   do last is actually the introduction. This is because you will
   write a much better introduction when you know what you
   actually wrote in the essay as a whole, and what your
   conclusions were. You are very unlikely to know these things
   before you start.

7. **Make an egg diagram!** What's this? I mentioned it earlier in
   the book, but didn't go into detail then. Try it now. Take a
   blank sheet of paper, laying it landscape in front of you. Now
   draw an egg, approximately normal size, in the middle of the
   page. Write inside the egg the title of the essay (or if it's a
   long title, just the key topic words).

8. **Now start drawing spokes round the egg, in different directions.** At the end of each spoke, write a short question – something that it may be worth addressing eventually in a paragraph in your essay. Questions including the following kinds of words and phrases are useful: 'Why does . . .?', 'What is . . .?', 'Who first found that . . .?', 'Where does . . . happen?', 'How does . . . work?', 'What else happens when . . .?' Before long, you'll have thought through all sorts of things that your essay might include.

9. **Now draw more spokes round the egg, in different directions.** This time put ideas at the end of each spoke. Just write two or three words – enough to remind you of each idea next time you see your diagram.

10. **Hatch your ideas and questions.** You can see now why it's called an 'egg diagram'! You can allow your thoughts to be 'free ranging' as you fill in your diagram. And you don't have to put them all down at this moment; you can return to your diagram and add more thoughts at any time later.

11. **Keep looking at the question in the middle of the egg before adding a new idea or question.** It's really important that *all* your ideas and questions relate to the central topic, so don't go working outwards making sub-sub-sub-sub-topic ideas or questions. Just about all the marks for your essay will be given for things that relate *directly* to the title or question as set.

12. **Don't hesitate to cross out ideas or questions, when you think of better ones.** This helps you to prioritize your thoughts and ensures that the essay will have only your best ideas in it – especially important if there's a tight word limit to work to. The messier an egg diagram becomes, the more thinking you've done, and the better your essay will turn out to be.

13. **Have your egg diagram with you in the next few lectures or classes relating to the subject.** Now and then you'll get more ideas or questions to add to your diagram. If you add them straight away, you've captured them. If you were to wait till you got back to your study den you could have forgotten the best of them!

14. **Keep your egg diagram where you can see it.** Pin it to a

wall or shelf in your own place, but continue to take it with you wherever you go, in case useful new ideas crop up and are worth adding to it.

15. **Poached eggs or scrambled eggs?** If you're working with fellow-students who are also using this idea, you can make *all* of your essays better by looking at each other's egg diagrams, and adding the best ideas from other people's diagrams to your own. This doesn't mean you'll end up writing identical essays (that would be dangerous) but it means you benefit from each other's planning.

16. **Keep talking to fellow-students about the topic.** Almost every time you do this, you'll find further ideas to add to your diagram to make it a better one.

17. **Find out for yourself that you can make egg diagrams in minutes, not hours.** It doesn't take long. A few minutes here and there is all it takes. And if you're doing this really early in the time-scale available to you there's no pressure on you. But you're saving yourself hours in the long run.

Shaping that Essay

We've already looked at how to get a lot of relevant ideas about that essay onto a single sheet of paper. The next stage is getting them into a sensible order. The following tips will help you to make your eventual essay flow well – and that's where a lot of the marks available are waiting for you to collect. Here goes...

1. **Sit back and admire your egg diagram.** You've by now got lots of questions that it will be worth addressing in your essay. You've also got lots of ideas that you can feed into answering your questions. But where to start? That's your next job.

2. **Don't actually start writing the essay yet!** There's more planning to do. Yes, the content of an essay does count, but so does the coherence, logical flow and so on. It's best to get the 'architecture' of your essay sorted out before you start joining the bricks together. Continue as follows.

3. **You've got lots of ideas and questions, but which are the most important?** Now is the time to look right round your egg diagram, and give each idea or question a star rating. For example, give things that are really central to the question as set a three-star *** rating, those that are quite important two stars**, and those that are only slightly relevant just one star *. Any that ended up with no stars can usually be safely crossed out now.

4. **Decide which idea, or question, will be the most**

sensible one to start your essay with. With a differently coloured pen or pencil, write a '1' beside that idea or question. It's likely to have one of your *** or ** ratings. Don't worry too much about getting it exactly right yet – you can always change it later.

5. **Where to go next?** Look at the question or idea you put a '1' beside, and look for something that leads on logically from that. Put a '2' beside this one. And so on. Don't go right round your egg diagram yet, just plan the order of the first half-dozen elements of it.

6. **Where to finish?** Sit back again and look at your diagram, this time looking for the idea or question that lends itself to being towards the very end of your essay. Put an 'X' (for 'exit point') beside this one with your coloured pen. Now look for the question or idea that leads naturally into your 'X' one. Put an 'X-1' beside this one – the penultimate idea or question. Go on to 'X-2' and 'X-3' and so on, planning the last few ideas which are going to round off your essay nicely in due course.

7. **Forget about the actual 'introduction' for now.** Your point '1' is just the first aspect of the topic that your essay is going to address. The introduction is actually much more important, but you can't write that well yet, as you still don't know what you'll eventually include in your essay, or what your conclusions are going to be. This is a perfectly healthy position to be in.

8. **Towards joined-up thinking?** Continue to work forwards from your points '1', '2', '3', and so on, and backwards from 'X', 'X-1' and 'X-2' and so on, until you've worked out a batting order for all your questions or ideas. This means you've made a provisional plan already not just for what the essay will contain, but also for the order in which you will present your arguments, discussions, and findings.

9. **A good plan is a flexible one.** Don't hesitate to cross out ideas that turn out not to be very good ones, and add better ones. If you think of an important new idea which fits nicely between '3' and '4' in your plan, add it in and call it '3a' and so on.

10. **NOW start your researching in earnest.** This means using your source materials to find out answers to your questions,

and information to include about your ideas. You don't have to do this researching all in one sitting! It's much better in fact to find out the answers to a couple of your questions today, another three tomorrow, and so on. Keep it manageable. You've still got plenty of time before you need to hand in the essay.

11. **Start assembling your information.** For example, jot down questions and answers on pieces of paper or cards, and keep them all in a plastic wallet or envelope for the time being. It can be useful to write the original number of the question or idea on each piece of paper you collect relating to that question.

12. **Keep looking at the original title or question.** More marks are lost for going off at a tangent to the question than for not knowing the answers. If you take your eyes off the title for too long, it seems to change, and when you look back at it, it isn't any longer exactly what you thought it was. Strange phenomenon!

13. **Check your brief yet again.** This time look particularly for any information you have about how many marks will be associated with particular aspects of the essay. Check once more any guidance you have about what is being looked for in a really good essay as compared to a less-good one, and so on. Make sure that you've addressed in your planning, as well as you can, the factors that are going to earn you top marks.

14. **Now you're ready to start your actual writing.** But don't plan to do it as a one-off marathon in a single sitting. If you started early, you should still have plenty of time left for drafting and redrafting. The tips in the next section go into this in more detail.

Drafting and Redrafting that Essay

Writing a perfect essay in a single go is not really a 'go-er' for most people. However, when writing essays during an exam, that's more or less what everyone has to try to do. We'll look at exam essays in another part of this book. That said, when you're writing a *coursework* essay, you can have as many tries as you choose to. The marks or grade you'll get are of course for your *final* version – but that may be a great deal better than your first one.

1. **Decide to start writing.** Just *thinking* about starting to write an essay doesn't actually earn you any marks. Get ready to write something – either with pen and paper or at your word processor. Now's not the time to have another look at the Internet, or to play that computer game, or to check your emails. Promise yourself one such thing as a reward only after you have done half an hour's worth of writing.

2. **Start somewhere in the middle!** For example, look at one of the ideas or questions where you've done a bit of researching, and know what you're going to say – just about that idea. Start with something you feel quite eager to get writing on. It can continue to be useful to use your numbering system, and write that number onto the sheet of paper (or type in '7: first try' as the heading of a new file, and save it as 'essay on [whatever] 7.1'.

3. **Aim to turn your idea or question into a single draft paragraph.** In your final essay, each paragraph should ideally

be about a single idea or question. If you find that you need more paragraphs, you've probably got more than one idea or question – or you're in danger of repeating yourself! Usually, the first sentence in any paragraph should be relatively short and focused, and say what the rest of the paragraph is going to be about. Sometimes, indeed, it is useful to start a paragraph with a question, then proceed to answer or discuss the question in the rest of the paragraph. In either case, a paragraph should be about one single idea or thought.

4. **Don't worry too much at this stage about the paragraph making sense!** It may be that it will only really make sense when read after the earlier parts of your essay, which you haven't yet drafted.

5. **Continue somewhat randomly turning your ideas or questions into paragraphs.** Gradually, accumulate pieces of paper with draft paragraphs (or separate computer files, or indeed a single file with different sections).

6. **When you've got most of the middle of your essay drafted, start thinking about links.** For example, look at what you've done for '7' and '8' and see how best to tweak the end of '7' so that it leads naturally into '8' (or tweak the beginning of '8' so that it follows on smoothly from '7').

7. **Next, work towards your ending.** It's again worth having a really good look at the question, and any other information you've got about the task in hand (such as assessment criteria, intended learning outcomes, briefings and so on). It is important that your essay is seen, at the end, to have really addressed the question.

8. **Now it's time to write the first draft of your introduction.** By now, you should have a good idea of what your essay will have covered, and how it will have gone about addressing the question. Remember that your introduction is the first thing that your assessors will see, and that first impressions are important. If the introduction reads really well, it sets up an expectation that it is going to be a good essay.

9. **Also spend time drafting and redrafting your ending.** This, of course, is the *last* thing your assessors will read – just before they start thinking about what mark or grade to give

your work. Clearly, it's best if your conclusion impresses them – and, indeed, lives up to the promises you made in your introduction.

10.   **Consider whether it's worth writing a completely new ending.** Sometimes, even after having come to a conclusion, it can be useful to end with a fairly short, tight, summary paragraph, summarizing how your essay has addressed the question, and repeating any main conclusions once more.

11.   **Put it all in a drawer for a week or two.** Clearly, you can only afford to do this if you did indeed get off to an early start. It's worth it, however, because when you read again the bits and pieces you've drafted, you'll often be able to make substantial improvements, as your subconscious mind will have continued to work away at the ideas you've written about.

12.   **When reading your essay drafts, read what you *wrote* and not just what you *meant*.** This takes conscious effort! It's all too easy to look at our words and see only what we *meant* to write. But your mark or grade will be awarded for what you actually *wrote*, not what you meant to write.

13.   **Don't throw anything away yet.** Whether working on a computer or with paper, continue to keep everything for the time being. The danger of throwing away earlier drafts is that on second thoughts you realize that one such draft was better than later ones. When working on a word processor, continue to save successive drafts using the 'save as' command, rather than overwriting each earlier version with the new one. Try to make it easy to track down which draft is which. It can be useful to put the date into the filename each time. Computers remember the dates in any case, but it's doubly safe to make the filenames speak for themselves in terms of what was written first and last.

14.   **Try reading parts out aloud to yourself.** You can of course do this mentally, but it's useful to *listen* in your mind to the words you have written. If you run out of breath reading one of your own sentences, it's clearly too long. Think about the key words in each sentence – the words you'd give emphasis to if reading them aloud. Check that these words on paper still carry the required degree of emphasis.

If they don't, look for replacement words that will do this better.

15. **Get the length about right.** You'll usually have a suggested word limit. It's best to get to within 10% or so of such a limit. This may well mean cutting things out. This is painful, especially when you've worked hard crafting your words, but there can be penalties (marks deducted!) for going too far over a word limit. If you happen to be *under* the word limit, it's usually not hard to expand a little on some of your paragraphs. If you're using a word processor, you'll be able to keep tabs on the length very easily. Word-count facilities are usually part of the 'Tools' menu in word-processing packages and are straightforward to use once you've practised using them.

16. **Get it all on paper now.** If you've been handwriting it, of course, it will already be on paper. But if you're word processing your essay, you may have done most of your drafting and redrafting on-screen. Research has shown that most people make at least some important and valuable changes to their writing only when seeing the whole thing printed out. Give yourself the chance to make such changes – print it all out and then do a bit more drafting and redrafting as above.

'I've started, so I'll finish!'

If you've put into practice all the tips in this section on writing essays, you'll now be within sight of finishing one off. We've already discussed why it's not a good idea to write either the very beginning or the final paragraph too early. There are, however, a few more things that are well worth doing as you prepare to polish up your masterpiece. Let's continue with the logical plan to get as many marks as you can for your work.

1. **Get as much feedback as you can on your work so far.** This means from other people. Who have you got to choose from? Fellow-students writing the same essay can give you really good feedback, but you've got to be a little careful now – you don't want them to steal too many of your ideas. Other people *not* writing the same essay can also give you useful feedback. In fact, almost any other pair of eyes on your work can be useful now.

2. **Take notice of the feedback you get.** Some of it won't be useful, and you can ignore it, but it's useful to identify *who* are the people who give you really helpful feedback, so that you can use them again. However, don't lean on other people in a one-sided way; try to reciprocate and give them useful feedback on their work.

3. **Don't wait too long for feedback.** Find out, by trial and error, who will give you *rapid* feedback. Feedback is all the more useful when you can still remember what you were trying to say in your essay.

4. **Ask for particular kinds of feedback.** For example, ask for suggested corrections to spelling and grammar. It's sometimes much easier for other people to notice your mistakes than it is for you to see them for yourself. Good copy-editors are worth their weight in gold at this stage.

5. **Get someone else to read it out to you.** Sometimes, when you hear your words read by someone who is coming to them afresh, you realize which parts are flowing well, and find out about any sentences that are harder for them to make sense of. Such sentences may in turn be harder for your assessors to interpret properly. When you *know* which sentences these are, you can do something about them.

6. **Now start polishing up that introduction again.** It's now your final opportunity to get your essay off to a really good start, to set up high expectations in whoever is going to assess it. Make sure that the introduction spells out clearly exactly where the essay is going to go. Now that *you* know exactly where it's going, this is relatively straightforward.

7. **Think again about the title.** Sometimes the title will be fixed, and there's nothing you can do about it. But if the final title is in your own control, now's the time to make it a good one. It can be productive to give yourself the task of composing half a dozen titles, and then choose the one that other people tell you sounds the most interesting.

8. **Polish your ending once again.** Try to make sure that if someone were to read *nothing but* your introduction and your conclusion, they'd have quite a good idea of what the whole essay was about. People marking your essay often go back and remind themselves of what you wrote by doing exactly that – having another look at the beginning and end, just before deciding what mark or grade to award your work.

9. **Now try *marking* your essay.** This is when it can be really useful to return to the exact briefing or instructions, especially if there is guidance on how many marks will go with each aspect of your essay. Check again any information you have about assessment criteria, particularly that relating to what is being looked for in a really good essay. Even at this late stage, it's useful to continue to add anything that makes your essay match the marking criteria as closely as you can.

10. **Continue to save and store your drafts as well as the final essay.** It's worth keeping all of your bits and pieces at least until the essay has been marked and returned to you. Your drafts are your best proof, should proof be needed, that it was indeed *you* who did the essay, and that you didn't download it from the Internet or steal other people's work.

11. **Choose when to hand in your essay for marking.** There's usually a deadline, so make sure it's handed in a little *before* the deadline. Don't leave it till the last minute – suppose you were ill on the day, or travel arrangements went wrong, or you forgot to take it with you! But don't hand it in *too* early either. It's frustrating finding yourself with a bright idea that you didn't include, too late to do anything because it's already handed in! A day or two early is about right, normally. And whatever you do, *don't* give it to someone else to hand in for you – however much you trust them.

12. **Let it go.** Once handed in, there's nothing further you can do to improve the mark or grade you will get. Don't have a post-mortem. Don't discuss that essay with everyone else who has done it too, or you'll just end up feeling depressed about all the good ideas *they* had which weren't in *your* essay – and they about yours – a vicious and unnecessary circle! Now's the time to move on to something else – you'll almost certainly have another task awaiting your attention.

Getting it Back – Marked!

This is the real final stage. It could be weeks after the date of handing it in. By the time you get it back, you may well have moved on to other topics in your course. However, doing the right things now can make a lot of difference to the *next* essay you write. Here are some suggestions.

1. **Decide to regard it as an important feedback opportunity.** If you really *want* to learn from whatever feedback you get, you're much more likely to make the most of it.
2. **Acknowledge that when you get your work back with a grade, your feelings may run high.** It's not unknown for a student to take a marked essay to a place outside, set fire to it, and then stamp on it! That may indeed make people feel better, but it's a lost learning opportunity (and could be dangerous, of course).
3. **Don't take too much notice of the mark or grade you're given.** There is, of course, nothing you can now *do* about whatever mark or grade you were given. The important thing is to learn about *why* you got whatever mark or grade you were given. This can help tremendously with your next essay.
4. **Don't become defensive.** It's all too easy to look at every critical comment as a personal affront. Remind yourself that any critical comments are about *what you wrote*, not about you

as a human being. You can change what you write next time. You don't have to try to change who you are!

5. **If your mark wasn't good, find out exactly why.** We learn at least as much through getting things wrong as we do through getting them right. And even if your mark was poor, look carefully for any clues regarding where you did score your marks.

6. **Don't be too smug if your mark or grade is good.** Try to work out *why* your work scored well. What did you do that pleased your assessors? How best can you put such things to work again in your next essay? And even if you did very well indeed, continue to look for what you might have done to make your work even better.

7. **Put it away for a while, then look at it again.** The real problem with feedback and marks together is that the marks cloud the picture. When your mind is full of thoughts about getting a high mark (or a low mark), you don't have room to really benefit from the feedback about your work. Once you've got used to whatever mark you were awarded, you will

find you are much better able to look dispassionately at the feedback, and get maximum value from it.

8. **Don't rest on your laurels.** 'Pride comes before a fall', and so on. If you got a really high mark or grade this time, the chances are that you'll have to work really hard to improve on it – or even to equal it again. Indeed, the chances are that your next mark won't be quite so good. Then you'll be disappointed, of course. But you can minimize that pain by learning as much as you can now about *why* you did well the first time.

9. **Analyse your mark or grade against the marking scheme.** Sometimes you'll have access to quite a lot of detail about how the marks were allocated for the essay. See where your work scored well alongside particular assessment criteria. More importantly, look at where you *didn't* score well. Try to work out *why* you missed particular marks. This will be really useful for next time.

10. **Try to look at the feedback fellow-students received too.** In fact, it's sometimes easier for you to make sense of the feedback comments on other people's work – you're not too close to that work to have your judgement clouded by emotions. At the same time, fellow-students may be able to give you useful insights into the real meaning of feedback comments written on your own work. Besides, looking at other people's marked essays tells you yet more about the overall 'rules of the game' regarding getting good marks for essays. The better you become acquainted with these rules, the more marks you can get next time – and indeed in exams too.

11. **Don't be afraid to seek clarification.** If you can't understand some of the feedback comments written on your work, find an appropriate time to ask about them. Be careful, however, not to appear as if asking for higher marks. And don't harangue your assessors in corridors or at the end of lectures. Don't make them feel as though their judgement is being challenged – that certainly doesn't help you to endear yourself to them! Make an appointment to see them, so that they have time to explain to you anything you *need* them to explain.

12. **Make yourself an action plan.** For each essay you have

marked, jot down three things to try to do again next time round, and three things to try to avoid in future. Then you can really let the essay go, regarding it as a useful learning experience, and hang on to your learning, rather than that mark or grade. Now file that essay, but keep your action plan.

Giving Due Credit

This is about giving due credit, in your own writing, to the ideas of others, and in particular getting your references exactly right. More importantly, it's about making sure you are not accused of plagiarism – which is very serious! Getting your references right is important in any assessed coursework that refers to the work of others. This is even more important if you write for publication (research papers, conference contributions, books and articles), when it's essential to be seen to be professional about referencing others' work – otherwise at best you'll have a lot of fiddling about to do to satisfy eagle-eyed editors, or at worst (more usually) they'll just reject your work.

1. **Know the relationship between 'citing' and 'referencing'.** 'Citing' is the way you refer in your own work to other people's published work. 'Referencing' is the related task where at the end of your own work you compile an exact and detailed list of the work you've cited, and is the hardest bit!

2. **Use the 'Harvard' ('name and date') system, whenever possible.** The Harvard system (as discussed below) is by far the most widely accepted one. However, if you're actually *asked* to use the alternative 'numeric' system, go along with it (but sooner or later you'll need to master the Harvard system anyway). The 'numeric' system puts superscript numbers next to authors' names ('Race[7] suggests. . . .') and then presents the references in numerical order at the end of the work.

3. **Be aware how fussy people are about citing and referencing!** In assessed coursework, you'll *always* lose marks if there is anything wrong with either. Journal editors or referees are particularly fussy, not least if you happen to be citing their own work in the subject, and getting the details wrong. External examiners can be really pernickety about referencing, not least as they are also likely to be journal editors or referees.

4. **Get into the habit of recording full details of the data you need to get your references exactly right.** It's best to do this at the time you use each article or source, and you'll save time when you refer to other people's work. You need to keep *all* of the following bits of information about every book or article:

    -   each author (and/or each editor): surnames, then initials;
    -   year of publication;
    -   exact title of article, book or chapter;
    -   the volume, part number and page numbers (particularly for journal articles) or place of publication: city, country; publisher.

    Some find it useful to use computer software to record and store such details, others keep boxes of small cards, one card for each source, with space for you to record carefully bits you may wish to quote directly in your own work.

5. **Find a recommended book or journal to use as a convenient example.** It's well worth having such a source to guide you until you become really familiar with citing and referencing. However, make sure the source you choose is doing it properly – there are plenty of books, journals and articles where citing and referencing are *not* done well. You can check your own sources by comparing how they handle references against advice contained in the tips below.

6. **Practise writing book references in the required form.** For example, the book containing these tips is:

    Race, P. (2003) *How to Study: Practical Tips for University Students.* Oxford, UK: Blackwell Publishing.

Another way of summarizing the Harvard style in general is:

> Author surname followed by comma, initials (year of publication in brackets) *Title of Book in Italics*. Place of publication, country: Publisher.

Look at the lists of references in your own textbooks and journal extracts to see how more complex sources are referred to.

7. **Be careful of the differences between articles and books.** The main difference is that for journal articles the article title is in normal print, and the *journal title* in italics, and that you need to include the volume number (and part number if appropriate) of the journal, and the page numbers of the article (but not details of the publisher or place of publication). For example:

> Hogwarts, D. and Alterio, M. (2004) Getting your references right when writing essays. *British Journal of Proper Writing* 93, 2: pp. 24–36.

8. **Make sure you remember what is going to be put into italics.** This is straightforward if you're using a word processor to store your details in the first place, but if you're in a library using a pen, it's easy to forget what to italicize later. One way round this is simply to *underline* in your handwriting the bits that will go in italics later.

9. **Get your in-text citing right too.** In your text, simply refer to author(s) and date as follows: 'Good advice on how to write references is given by Hogwarts and Alterio (2004) who suggest that . . .'. Alternatively, if you're making a direct quotation from your chosen source, this could be duly indented as follows:

> It is really important for students to pay due attention to precise referencing, particularly when quoting directly from the work of others. (Hogwarts and Alterio, 2004)

10. **Use 'et al.' appropriately.** '*Et al.*' is short for '*et alia*', which

in Latin means 'and others'. When there are several authors involved in an article or book, it would be clumsy to list them all every time you cited their work. When there are only two names to consider, use both, as in the examples shown previously. But when there are three or more authors (such as in the historic *Taxonomy of Educational Objectives*) you could refer to it as (Bloom *et al.*, 1956) in the body of your work, but would need to give the full reference in your list at the end. In this case, it is:

Bloom, B. S., Engelhart, M. D., Furst, E. J., Hill, W. H. and Krathwohl, D. R. (1956) *Taxonomy of Educational Objectives: Cognitive Domain.* New York: McKay.

Note that you may have to look twice to work out exactly whose initials go with their family names! With references involving several names, one of the most common mistakes is not having written down somewhere all the *later* names in the list, and this can result in a great waste of time and frustration when putting together your final list. Note also that some publishers prefer Latin abbreviations such as '*et. al.*', '*op. cit.*' and '*ibid.*' to be set in roman type rather than italic.

11. **Try to avoid some of the other 'jargon' abbreviations.** For example, '*op. cit.*' is sometimes used to refer again to work that has already been cited, and '*ibid.*' or '*idem*' can be used to mean 'in the same source referred to above', but for most practical purposes it is easier simply to refer afresh to the source. Look at your own source materials in your own subject area to see whether such abbreviations are often used by other writers.

12. **Take particular care with 'compound' references.** This is when (for example) you're referring to the work of particular authors contained in a chapter of an edited collection (for example, conference proceedings). An example of a correctly expressed compound reference is given below:

Lucas, L. and Webster, F. (1998) Maintaining standards in higher education? A case study. In Jary, D. and Parker, M. (eds), *The New Higher Education: Issues and Directions for the*

Post-Dearing University. Stoke-on-Trent, UK: Staffordshire University Press, pp. 105–13.

13. **Note the commonly used variants on the Harvard system.** For example, some books or journals put the author (or editor) names in BLOCK CAPITALS. Also, the place of publication is sometimes put last, instead of after the title. Some publishers expect the first letter of each word of the title to be put in upper case, and others don't! If you're writing for a particular journal or publisher, it's well worth conforming exactly to the expected house style. The important point is to aim for consistency of style.

14. **Newspaper articles need references too.** For example, if you're referring to a news item or article in *The Guardian*, your in-text reference of, say, (Jones, 2003) would need the full reference, with exact date of publication and page numbers, in your alphabetical list at the end of your work:

> Jones, J. (2003) Students sent down for plagiarism, *The Guardian*, 31 January, 24–5.

15. **Put your list of references in alphabetical (and where necessary date) order.** This means in fact in alphabetical order of the family names of the first-named author. When you include an author more than once, you need to arrange the references in date order too, for example:

> Smith, A. (1997) . . .
> Smith, A. (2000) . . .
> Smith, A. (2002) . . .

In cases where you have cited more than one source by a particular author in a given year, you need to show which is which, by including letters in the dates, as follows:

> Smith, A. (2000a) . . .
> Smith, A. (2000b) . . .

and in such cases when you cite their work in your text you need to use (Smith, 2000a) and so on.

16. **Web-based sources need references as well!** Author and title details are as for journal articles, but this time you need to include the Uniform Resource Locator (URL) of the source, e.g. http://www.leeds.ac.uk/students/study.htm (accessed 20 July 2003). The date that the reference was seen is included so that if the website address changes, it might be possible for the reader to track down where the reference is now stored (or whether it is no longer available).

17. **Do a careful check, just of the citing and referencing, when finishing off your work.** Whether you're preparing your work for assessment, or sending it off to a prospective publisher, it's important to make time to check this aspect really carefully. In particular, check that each source you've cited is indeed included in the references, *and* that you haven't included in the references any source that you subsequently deleted from your citations.

Part IV

Presentations

Preparing Your Presentation

'Presentation' starts with the letter 'P'. So do the three important stages leading you to being able to give a good one. The stages are:

- preparation;
- practice;
- performance!

We'll look systematically at each of these in the tips that follow.

Few students survive college nowadays without giving a presentation in one form or another. For example, you may be required to give a solo or joint presentation as part of your course. This may, indeed, be an assessed component of your course. In any case, it's good for you! Preparing and giving a presentation will be useful experience, and will undoubtedly help you later in giving good interviews when job-hunting and so on. Preparing well for a presentation makes all the difference, so I'll share some tips with you on this first, and then we'll move on to actually giving your presentation.

1. **'What sorts of presentation might I have to prepare?'**
   There is quite a range. For example, you might be asked to lead a seminar, with a relatively small group of students. In your final year, you may be asked to give a presentation on, for example, a research project that in its own right was a significant element in your course. The presentation may be assessed by lecturers, and possibly peer-assessed by your fellow-students.

2. **Don't get stressed out about it.** For some people, preparing and giving a presentation is as easy as falling off a log. For others, it seems terrifying. For most people, it's somewhere in between. The *first* time you prepare a presentation is likely to be a steep learning curve. Like most things, it becomes a lot easier the more you do it – but there's got to be a first time for everyone for everything.

3. **Take action if there's any genuine reason why you *shouldn't* be asked to give a presentation at all.** For example, if you've got a severe speech impediment – or can't speak at all – it would be unreasonable to expect you to prepare and give a presentation. However, it would be perfectly reasonable to ask you to *prepare* one, but not give it. If it's an assessed presentation, and you can't actually give it, it should be possible to negotiate with your lecturers an alternative assessment, in keeping with your particular needs. But don't regard being *terrified* as sufficient reason not to be asked to give your presentation – you won't get far with that one!

4. **Even if you're worried about it, stop worrying and get started on your preparations.** Half the fear is of starting off the whole business of getting ready to give a presentation, and once you're under way with this you'll feel a lot better about it. In any case, you're likely to feel more relaxed about it the more you find out about the topic. And doing something useful is a better use of your time and energy than sitting there brooding about it!

5. **Find out how long it's intended to be.** There is usually quite a tight time limit, whether it is a seminar you're leading, or a formal presentation. Once you know how long you'll need to talk, you can start planning sensibly for what you will say.

6. **Find out whether you're just giving a talk, or leading in to a question-and-answer session afterwards.** Usually, you'll be doing both. Obviously, if you're going to answer questions on your presentation, you'll need to know more about it than if you're just giving a short talk.

7. **Find out what the topic is going to be.** Sometimes you'll have the chance to choose your own topic. If you're giving a presentation on work you've done as a project, for example, your topic will already be defined to some extent (though you

would be wise to choose only *part* of the project to address in your presentation). Alternatively, you may simply be allocated a topic about which to prepare a presentation, for example as part of a student seminars schedule.

8. **Find out more about your audience.** How many people will be there? Will they be fellow-students only, or will one or more lecturers also attend? Will you already know all of the people there, or could there be people 'from outside' – employers, research students, etc.?

9. **If it's an *assessed* presentation, check out how many marks it's worth.** It may just be a pass/fail element. It probably doesn't count for a substantial proportion of coursework credit. Keep your efforts in proportion with the potential marks. For example, don't spend months preparing a really excellent presentation, then failing a vital exam because you *should* have been spending most of that time on your revision.

10. **Do your research.** This is, of course, one of the *reasons* for having presentations as part of a course – they *cause* you to get down to some research. This will be useful practice for skills you will need sooner or later in any case.

11. **Track down what you need to know about the subject.** Often, you'll be helped by lecturers here. They may suggest particular source materials – books, articles, websites and so on. Whatever *else* you do, follow up their suggestions first.

12. **Keep careful track of the sources you find.** You will need the exact references for each of your sources when you give your presentation. The best time to get these details is when you're using the particular books, journals or websites. A week or two later you may not be able to find them again if you don't capture their details – authors, dates, page numbers, URLs for websites, and so on. See the set of tips on 'Giving due credit', which is about how exactly to collect and store such details.

13. **Find out what facilities you'll be able to use when you give your presentation.** For example, you may be able to use a blackboard or whiteboard, or a flipchart, or an overhead projector or a computer with data projector to display a PowerPoint presentation (or 'show') – or any combination of such things.

14. **Find out whether you're expected – or allowed – to give copies of a handout to your audience.** You may even be allowed a modest amount of photocopying to make these – though you're more likely to have to pay for copies yourself.

15. **Plan out your overheads or slides, and your handouts, if you're using any of these.** Once you know what your audience is going to see, you're in a much better position to plan what you're going to *say* about these things during your presentation.

16. **Make your script or notes.** It helps most people to write down at least a rough version of what they're going to say. Alternatively, you may prefer to have a list of bullet points or headings, and expand on these in turn without having written a script.

17. **Plan out how you can involve your audience.** Most good presentations include parts where the presenter asks the audience some questions. This takes up some time of course, but can be well worth it.

18. **Do some practice runs.** Look at the next-but-one set of tips for some of the things you should aim to do on the day of your presentation, and practise them until you become confident about doing them. In particular, however, practise the timing. If it's a 10-minute talk plus 10 minutes of questions and answers, you should aim to come to your final point in *exactly* ten minutes, ready for questions. This takes some doing, but is well worth striving for – others might not manage this one! For more on practising see below.

19. **Meanwhile, if you're going to use audio-visual aids to support your presentation, look at the next set of tips for advice on how to make the most of them.** You may be planning to use one or more out of the following list: blackboard, whiteboard, flipchart, overhead projector or data projector to support your presentation. Each of these can be used well – or used badly! The following tips will help to point you in the right direction.

Preparing Your Visual Aids

Whether or not you use low-tech or high-tech visual aids to support your presentation will depend on several factors – how long it is, what sort of subject you're going to be talking about, and whether it is relatively 'normal' to be expected to use such things. If you're not going to use visual aids, skip these tips, and get straight on to the suggestions about practising. But if you *are* going to use them, you might as well make a good job of it, so check through the following tips to see if there is any fine-tuning you can do which will help you to make an even better impression. We'll start with the simple visual aids, and work towards the more-complex ones. Some of the same principles continue to apply.

1. **If you're using a blackboard, use it well.** Don't talk to the board while you're writing things on it. Write fairly high up on the board, otherwise people at the back may not be able to see what you're writing. After you've written something on the board, make sure you're not obstructing your audience's view of it. Don't rub anything off before people have had a chance to see it! Write fairly big, so that your writing can be clearly read by the people sitting at the back. And make sure you have some chalk and an eraser on your person, especially on the day itself.

2. **If you're using a whiteboard, most of the same things apply.** But more importantly, use the right kind of pens. These should be of the 'dry-wipe' variety. Water-soluble pens are more risky, but will do, provided you've got something wet

to clean the board. Check that they *do* rub out completely. Whatever you do, don't use permanent pens, or flipchart pens, or indelible markers and so on. These *won't* rub off the whiteboard, and this will make you unpopular, not to say infamous!

3. **Clean the overhead projector if you're going to use it.** The 'platen' (the glass plate on which you put your transparencies) may well need cleaning – use a damp tissue. Similarly the lens or mirror may be dusty, and your transparencies will look a lot nicer if you clean these too.

4. **Set up the overhead projector properly.** Find out how it works (not least where the on–off switch or lever is – there are many different kinds of projector!). Find out how to focus it well. Find out how to use the 'fringe control' to remove blurry coloured edges to the image. These controls work differently on different machines.

5. **Make sure the screen is in a sensible position.** Sometimes you'll have no choice – it could be a pull-down screen, or a white part of a roller-board. Shiny whiteboards don't make very good screens – a blank wall may be better. Ideally, the screen should be where everyone can see it without obstruction – particularly without *you* as an obstruction.

6. **Find somewhere you can put your papers and transparencies.** A small table beside the projector is useful, but many projectors have fold-up 'shelves' on one or both sides. However, there's not a lot of room on these shelves, and slides tend to fall off.

7. **Make your transparencies readable!** Nowadays, it's relatively straightforward to produce transparencies from a computer or a photocopier, if you have the right kinds of film, and you can then make them look good, and indeed colourful. However, handwritten transparencies can still be effective. In either case, the main thing that spoils them is the writing or print being too small to be read at the back of the room – you'll no doubt have experienced exactly this in some lectures!

8. **Get to know PowerPoint if you're making transparencies from your computer.** You can use PowerPoint simply to make transparencies – you don't have to

go the whole hog and make a PowerPoint presentation to run through a data projector. PowerPoint slides can look much better than anything you are likely to make using just a word-processor. And even if you *are* turning your slides into a slide-show, you can print them off onto transparency film so that you've got a good back-up if the technology should not be available – or lets you down on the day.

9. **Use mostly the top half of the screen.** With transparencies, you can slide up the film so that the part you want your audience to see is high up on the screen. With PowerPoint presentations run through a data projector, however, you can't do this, and it can be useful to quite deliberately just use the top half of slides.

10. **If you're going in for PowerPoint slide-show presentations, remember you'll need to set it all up.** At best, you simply slip a floppy disk or CD into an existing machine, and your show is on the screen in seconds. But there may not *be* a computer – or a projector – or a remote control – or a mouse – or any power! If you're using PowerPoint for your presentation, it's good insurance to print three-slides-per-page or six-slides-per-page handouts as well, so that you can at least use the materials you've prepared if you can't get your show on the screen on the day.

11. **Check out whether there will be any technical support on the day.** For an important series of presentations, such support may well be lined up, and this can take a lot of the worry out of the technical side of your presentation when you're using complex media. You may well be perfectly capable of being your own technician, but when you're preoccupied with giving a good presentation, it is better not to have to worry about the technology too.

12. **The joy of PowerPoint is that it's so easy to edit and improve your presentation.** It takes much longer to make a new set of transparencies – and is much more expensive too. So balance the benefits against the risks, in the context of your own presentation, and consider the facilities and technical support available to you.

Practising Your Presentation

As with most things, practice makes perfect. But perhaps not? Look at your lecturers, for example. *Some* of them may be excellent at lecturing – which is at least partly related to giving presentations – others aren't! But they're all reasonably practised. So let's focus on the right *kinds* of practice, so that your presentation can be as good as you can reasonably make it, without it taking over your life.

1. **Get used to the sound of your voice.** It can help to practise in an empty classroom – of the sort in which you may eventually do your presentation. But anywhere will do, so long as you can practise talking, without feeling embarrassed.

2. **Practise using any visual aids you've decided to use for your presentation.** If you've used the tips given earlier to help you design such aids, it's worth making sure that you give the appearance of using them well and effortlessly, to further enhance the overall impression made by your presentation.

3. **Find out approximately how much you can say in a given number of minutes.** This is really only discovered by trying it out. You may be surprised either way! Sometimes it takes far longer than you might imagine to talk through what's on a single sheet of paper. At other times, especially if you're nervous, you may speak much faster, and get through it in much *less* time than you'd expected. Since timing is so important in most presentations, it's worth making sure that you have about the right amount to say.

4. **Plan your introduction carefully.** This is where you make your first impression on your audience, and you want that to be a good one. It's where you explain what the presentation will be about, and perhaps *how* you plan to go about it.

5. **Practise your introduction.** This is the bit where you'll probably say who you are, and a few words telling your audience what you're going to be talking about – and possibly *why* they may be interested in what you're going to cover. It's particularly useful to be so practised at getting into your introduction that you will become able to do it on auto-pilot, rather than allowing yourself to feel tense as you start your presentation.

6. **Have 'extras' up your sleeve.** When you come to your actual presentation, you could end up speaking rather faster than you normally would, in the heat of the moment perhaps. Then, if you find yourself with not enough to fill the allotted minutes, it can be really useful to have one or two extra points to slip in – for example expanding a little on something you've already mentioned.

7. **Have 'escape lanes' ready too.** For one reason or another, you might run out of time when your real presentation comes around. You might, for example, get off to a late start because someone before you overran. Or there may be an interruption or question you hadn't bargained for. It's well worth avoiding trying to rush through everything you intended to say when you haven't got time to say it all. Therefore, have some things that you can miss out (with no one noticing) if you find time is creeping up on you. But make sure, of course, that it isn't your carefully planned *ending* that you sacrifice.

8. **Practise until you don't simply have to read out your presentation.** Once you've got some practice in, you will find you can talk quite naturally just using a list of key points – which may well be the points you prepared on slides or overheads.

9. **Practise your ending.** Whatever else happens in a presentation, it's important that it comes to a good solid ending. Don't just stop! Don't let your presentation fizzle out. End with a bang! Make it clear that you're coming to some conclusions. Practise looking up at your audience (who aren't

yet there, of course) and saying 'Thank you' as your last two words. Or 'Thank you. Now are there any questions you'd like me to try to answer, please?' And so on.

10. **Now go public.** If you've got some friends who are also preparing to give presentations, see if you can arrange to practise with each other. This can be a lot more fun than just talking to yourself, and you'll probably learn a lot from watching how they go about it. You'll notice things where you think 'Ah, that's working well. I'll try to do that in my own presentation too', and also where you think 'Oh no, I must try to make sure I *don't* do that in my presentation.'

11. **Keep watching how other people go about it.** Watch your lecturers with renewed interest. Note the things that they do to keep their audiences engaged. Note the things they do that bore their audiences rigid. Jot down during lectures some reminders to yourself about what you're going to do (and going to avoid!) in *your* presentation.

12. **Practise answering questions.** This is where it can be *really* helpful to involve your friends. Get them to quiz you after your practice runs. Quiz them after theirs. You'll gradually get more comfortable responding to questions. This sort of practise is not only relevant to answering questions after your presentation, it is also good preparation for interviews, or even oral exams or 'vivas'.

13. **Make your own questions too.** You could write these on cards, then 'draw' a card, and respond to the question, in random order. Work out which questions you find it easier to answer. Find out which questions are more difficult to answer, and perhaps do some further research to make you better placed to answer these.

Performing on the Day

Now the day has come. You've already polished up your overheads or slides. You've prepared copies of the handout (if you're using one). You've got yourself to the room where you're going to do your presentation. Only a few minutes to go, and that particular presentation will be history – you'll have done it. If it's your *first* presentation, you'll never have another, the next one will be your *second* one, which is much easier. Here goes.

1. **Get there early.** You may, of course, be there already, following on from someone else who's just given a presentation. If not, or if you're first, spare yourself any anxiety, and be there in time to get yourself settled.

2. **Check any equipment you're using.** If you're using an overhead projector, for example, get it into the right place, focus it properly, and try it out so you know where the various controls are. In particular, find out how to switch it on or off. If you're doing something more ambitious, such as using PowerPoint slides, you'll need to spend longer checking out the facilities, until they're all second nature to you.

3. **Keep calm while your audience take their places.** It sometimes helps to chat to whoever is first there, especially if you already know them, until everyone is in place. As you do this, make sure that you can see a clock or your watch. Perhaps take your watch off and place it beside your notes, so that you can keep an eye on the time without anyone noticing you do so.

4. **Get ready to start, note your actual start-time (perhaps jotting it down so you don't forget when you started), then start!** Start boldly but quite slowly. If you feel your voice going up towards the squeaky register, bring it back down again. Say who you are, what the title of your presentation is, and a little about what you're going to cover in the next few minutes.

5. **Keep eye-contact with members of your audience**. Don't just stare at your notes, or the floor, or the ceiling, or the walls, or the image on the screen, or out of the window. None of these is judging your presentation.

6. **Don't worry if eye contact seems hard.** With a little practice, you can appear to be looking at members of your audience when you're actually looking *past* them into the distance. This is still much better than not looking in their direction at all.

7. **Take encouragement from your audience.** When people are interested, some will nod their agreement at things you say, some will smile, and so on. All presenters tend to do better when there's a nodder in the audience – watch how your lecturers react to this.

8. **Watch your audience's reactions.** For example, if you've slipped in a little humour, but not even a twitch of a smile is discernible on anyone's face, don't include any more humour in that presentation. If, however, they *love* it, give them some more. Watch how comedians play to an audience, and take their cues from each different audience.

9. **Divert people's attention if you find yourself feeling really nervous.** For example, if you're using overheads or PowerPoint slides, the moment you put up a slide, everyone's gaze switches from you to the screen. This gives you the opportunity to recompose yourself, or scratch your nose, or indeed remind yourself just where you've got to in your presentation, and think about what you're going to say next.

10. **Don't read out to people things they can read for themselves.** People don't like being read to! Besides, if you're showing a slide with bullet points on it, for example, they will be able to read them a great deal faster than you

could speak them. Similarly, if you've prepared a handout, don't just read things out of it – instead direct their attention to (for example) 'near the top of page two . . .' if you want to refer them to something in the handout.

11. **Work towards your planned conclusion.** Take your planned escape roads if time is running out, and miss out some parts of what you could have covered, but don't miss out the conclusion. If there's more time than you expected, slip in one or two of the extras you have up your sleeve.

12. **Conclude on time.** If it's supposed to be a 10-minute talk, and you finish in exactly 10 minutes from when you started, it all looks that bit more professional, better prepared and so on.

13. **Open it up for questions.** Sometimes you may have the help of a chairperson, who picks which questioner will pose the next question and so on. Or perhaps it will all be up to you, and people wishing to ask questions will raise a hand. Try to take questions in the order people indicated that they would like to ask them.

14. **When you *know* how to answer a question, take your time.** The longer you can talk about the things you know well, the less time you'll have to try to talk about things you *don't* know. Watch how politicians do this when interviewed on TV – if they're talking about something they *want* to talk about they sometimes don't let the interviewer get a word in edgeways. But don't be *so* rude!

15. **When you're asked a question you can't answer, don't waffle.** Give yourself time to think first. One subtle way of doing this is to repeat the question for everyone's benefit, for example if people at the back may not have heard a question asked by someone at the front. It's surprising how much thinking you can do in the few seconds it takes for you to repeat a question! Alternatively, *clarify* the question. Ask the questioner, 'Is what you're asking . . .' and explain what you think they're asking for.

16. **If you *really* can't answer a question, say so.** Only do this, of course, after clarifying the question, and deciding that there's nothing sensible you can say in reply. Sometimes it's worth then throwing the question back to the questioner:

'Why do *you* suppose it is that so and so happens?' Or think of opening it up to other members of the audience, especially if you can see from their body language that someone is itching to jump in and answer the question.

17. **If you're chairing your own questions, keep an eye on the time.** When your allotted time for questions is coming to an end, say (for example), 'There's time for one more question now'. After answering that one, look up, smile and say something like 'Thank you for your questions', and start tidying up your notes to leave the presentation spot.

18. **The presentation's now over, but your learning isn't quite over.** After you've given a presentation, it's well worth spending a little time reflecting on it. Jot down what you learned about giving a presentation, and some small action points for next time you find yourself in the same situation. What would you do differently next time? What worked well,

that you would do exactly the same next time? And so on. Reflecting on your presentation helps you to get it out of your system.

19. **Gain any feedback you can about your presentation.**
When you later meet people who have been in your audience, pick your moment and ask them structured questions such as, 'What did you like about my presentation?' or 'What do you think was the least successful part of my presentation?' You'll learn more from their answers to such questions than if you'd simply asked them 'What did you think of my presentation?'

20. **Continue to watch other people's presentation tactics.**
Once you've given your own presentation, you're actually much more receptive. Having been through it yourself, you're more able to notice things that people do well – or badly.

Part V

Ups and Downs

Peaks and Troughs

You're not a robot. Sometimes you may wish you were, and that everything around you was straightforward and orderly, but life's not like that. The important thing is *coping* – with both the highs and lows of being a human being. A later set of tips looks in more detail at coping with disappointments, but for now we'll just concentrate on the more general side of the upwards and downwards swings of feelings that are part of normal life. Facing up to peaks is sometimes a bit challenging, but most of the tips below are about the other side of the picture – coping well with troughs.

1. **Accept that you'll have both peaks and troughs.** Don't believe for a moment that there's anything wrong with you just because one day seems quite different from another.
2. **Don't regard any trough as being too deep to climb out of.** It may indeed feel deep the first moment you're in it, but once you're out of it, it will seem far less significant. Practise training your mind to take a helicopter view of such uncomfortable situations, as if looking at yourself dispassionately from a height, and putting the situation into perspective.
3. **When in a deep trough, don't be too proud to seek help.** There are lots of people around you who can help if and when needed, including at least some of your friends and fellow-students, as well as family and tutors. There are skilled helpers such as counsellors, helplines, and so on, too. Simply

putting your trough into words to explain to someone can often help you to rationalize it sufficiently to begin to climb out of it by yourself.

4. **A stranger can sometimes help more than a friend.** The advantage of a 'stranger' – perhaps a counsellor, doctor or other professional – is that once you've worked through your problem with their help, you don't ever need to talk to them again if you don't wish to. This can be more comfortable than sharing your problems too deeply with a close friend or family member, and then feeling embarrassed about it when it's all over.

5. **Avoid transferring blame.** There's little mileage in allocating blame for any unsatisfactory situation in which you find yourself. It may not be your fault at all; it may be no one's fault at all; indeed it may entirely be someone else's fault, but just deciding whose fault it is doesn't get you out of your trough.

6. **Avoid thoughts which begin with 'if only . . .'.** Such thoughts tend to be unproductive. They don't solve things. Whatever your situation, live with the art of the possible. Think creatively about what you *can do* about it.

7. **When you're in a hole, stop digging!** In your earnest endeavours to get out of the hole, don't go and make it even deeper. Now is the time to do something else. Find something useful to do, that's not too hard. The hole won't get deeper by itself meantime . . .

8. **. . . But it could fill up with water!** Don't leave a trough unattended for *too* long. While it's often useful to step away from it and do something else, it's important to get back to that trough when you're ready to do something about it. More about this soon.

9. **Make the most of each peak.** When you feel you're being particularly productive and efficient, and *enjoying* such feelings, forge ahead. Earn yourself some spare time for later. But don't forge ahead doing unimportant or irrelevant things, even when tempted. Use the energy of your peak to get even further ahead with important things that are central to your future studies.

10. **Pace yourself.** Don't peak too early. While it's very

understandable, when you're a new student, to put everything you've got into proving that you're up to the new challenges around you, you really need to save enough energy so that you have it available when it matters. If you burn yourself out too early, you won't do yourself justice later – for example when exams become important.

11. **Break your workload into manageable chunks.** Even if you're in a trough, there will be some useful little chunks of work that you can still face and get on with perfectly satisfactorily, even when not feeling on top form. You may reasonably choose to defer more demanding tasks for later at such times.

12. **Make the most of your fellow-students.** For example, when you do at least some of your work as part of a small group of like-minded students, you can share the peaks and troughs, and support each other through both. Often, simply discussing your trough with fellow-students can make it seem a lot less daunting.

13. **Don't hide your feelings from yourself.** We would all prefer to appear to be constant, steady and balanced at all times. Indeed we may wish to – and choose to – hide some of our feelings (whether of despair or elation) from other people, but it remains important to face up to our own feelings. It's permissible to feel angry, frustrated, discouraged and 'down', just as much as it is to feel elated, stimulated, 'fired' and enthused. Human beings are a feeling species.

14. **Use both peaks and troughs as learning experiences.** During or after each kind of extreme, spend a few minutes objectively analysing what you're learning from each experience. There will often be tangible learning outcomes – things you can apply to help you gain the most from your next peak, or help you through your next trough.

15. **Make time to have peaks and troughs.** Get ahead of schedule. Simply *being* ahead of schedule makes for feeling good about your life. But more importantly, when you're ahead of schedule, you're much less vulnerable to troughs – you've got time for them. This can mean that you don't get them anyway!

16. **Become a juggler.** Get good at having several balls in the air

at any one time. Don't concentrate for too long on any one thing – be it your studies, or life in general. When you have several things going on, you can choose which one of them you're going to concentrate on for the immediate time ahead, and you can select something *manageable* that you can do for the next short hour, rather than feel stopped in your tracks because there's one thing you just can't face doing yet.

Managing Disappointments

Sometimes things just don't turn out as you would have wished them to turn out! Elsewhere in this book we've looked at the value of learning from mistakes, and in the previous set of tips we explored coping with peaks and troughs in particular. Disappointment may be part of the picture in such cases, but in the next two sets of tips we're looking at disappointments, a particular kind of trough – whether or not any mistakes were actually made. Perhaps you don't get the grade or mark expected, or you reckon you deserved. Or you don't get the credit for your share of some work you did in a group. Or someone says 'no' when you ask them a question you really wanted them to say 'yes' to. Or you trusted someone and they let you down. Or you made a sound suggestion or proposal and it was turned down. Or you didn't succeed in an interview and didn't get the job you really wanted. We all have to cope with disappointments now and then. But perhaps we need to do *more* than just cope?

Let's look at ways we can *manage* our disappointments. These tips work best when you've got a particular disappointment to work your way round. Don't go looking for one, however; save these tips for when you need them. In the first set of tips that follow, we'll look at ways of coming to terms with a disappointment, then in the next set we'll explore some ways of getting over it.

1. **Check first that you really have a disappointment.** If you're simply disappointed that someone else didn't do something in particular, that doesn't really count – you don't

actually *own* that sort of disappointment. When you *really* have
a disappointment to deal with, it's much closer than someone
else letting you down – it could even be about *you* feeling
you've let yourself down.

2. **Check next the scale of your disappointment.** They come
    in many shapes and sizes. They're accompanied by many
    different emotions depending on the circumstances. The tips
    below span a wide range of possibilities; *your* disappointment
    is likely to link directly to only some of these, so it will be
    useful to look through the rest of these tips and be really
    selective – choose and use the tips that are likely to be directly
    useful to you.

3. **Don't pretend, even to yourself, that it doesn't hurt.**
    Disappointments often hurt. In fact, they usually hurt. You
    may not want to show other people how much you're hurt,
    but you can be honest with yourself.

4. **Don't keep turning the disappointment over in your
    mind till you become bitter or cynical.** That won't
    improve the situation – and indeed can make it feel worse. It

is indeed useful and sensible to analyse the situation during your journey out of the feelings of disappointment, but only so long as you're still gaining insight into what you can do in the future to minimize that particular sort of disappointment happening again, or hitting you so hard, should it happen again.

5. **Console yourself that you're in good company.** Everyone around you has had disappointments. Everyone will have further disappointments in the future. So will you. The present one is very unlikely to be the biggest disappointment in your entire life. Get real about it! And if it *really* is? Well then, cheer up, you're one of the elite few who have already had their very worst disappointment, and life will get better from now on!

6. **Recognize that at least part of your feelings are a form of grief.** You've lost something, even though it may only have been something you didn't ever have. You've lost a chance, an opportunity, a particular hope. You've missed out on a particular target or ambition. But with a genuine disappointment, all the grieving in the world can not turn the tables and give you exactly what it was that you wanted. There may be a next time, or perhaps not. So don't grieve for too long.

7. **Probe your emotions further:** *how* **do you feel disappointed?** There may be one or more of several things going on in your mind. You may be *angry* – for example at an injustice, or angry with yourself. You may be *depressed*, perhaps at the thought of not feeling able to reach a target you'd set yourself – or not reaching standards other people expect of you. You may be *afraid* – for example that you may fail, or won't be able to cope, or that you will let other people down. It's useful to sort out your particular mix of emotions, then to tackle each one in the most appropriate way, as follows:

   • **if you're angry:** are you angry at other people, or at yourself? If the latter, it's relatively straightforward to plan how in future not to make yourself so angry with yourself. You may have to be more reasonable about what you should expect from yourself. Similarly, other people. You might want to put the system right – for yourself next time, or for other people in the same situation.

- **if you're depressed:** this is most likely to be due to the consequences of your disappointment. You may be able to improve on these consequences – at least next time a similar situation arises.
- **if you're afraid:** you may do well to think about what you can do to minimize the future effects of your fear – possibly about how to raise your own performance levels beyond the fear level.

8. **Probe deeply now: *why* are you so disappointed?** Let's take the case of someone who didn't get a top job he really wanted. It turned out (after being painfully disappointed for what seemed like a long time) that he didn't really want to *do* that top job, he simply wanted to *be* that top person. That's why disappointments sometimes hurt a lot – they're often about not *being* something rather than not simply having something, or not having the chance to do something. But we can't all always *be* everything we all want to be. Sometimes, in fact, what we want to *be* is, to put it bluntly, just beyond our capability – we *can't* be everything we want to be. But that's no bad thing – there's no harm in over-ambition, except that we risk disappointments more often. It's better to *want* and not always to *get*, than never to want!

9. **Face up to the humiliation.** That's often what causes the real pain associated with a disappointment. Sometimes it's quite easy to accept not being able to have something, or do something, or even be something, but it's harder to cope with other people seeing that such is the case. How many other people? Remind yourself that the vast majority of the population of planet Earth have absolutely no idea you've had that disappointment – nor, indeed, would they think twice about it if they were told about it. Humiliation? The scale is actually quite limited.

10. **Be logical about any injustice you feel you've had done to you.** Many disappointments are associated with injustices. Sometimes the injustice is very real – for example if you did an excellent piece of work, but got a poor grade, or if you

were by far the best candidate for the job and someone else got it. However, the fact remains that such elements of injustice are often quite irreversible. If you were to make a fuss, the decision would remain the same (and you'd risk further embarrassment). In such circumstances, the only safe thing to do is to let the injustice go – don't hang on to feeling bad about it or you'll just end up damaging yourself and no one else.

11. **Get past the 'I wish I hadn't done that!' reaction.** If the disappointment is linked to an exam you didn't pass because you didn't revise for it, or a job you didn't get because you said silly things at the interview, or a person you didn't impress because you took entirely the wrong approach – accept that it's *happened* now. The only value of 'I wish I hadn't done that!' is that you'll know better what to do in the next set of similar circumstances. The learning pay-off is useful and significant. This 'if only I . . .' agenda is virtual. Once you have worked that out, it's time to translate it from the past tense to the future tense: 'Next time I'm in this situation, I'm going to try to . . .'.

12. **Go beyond wallowing.** Every disappointment can be regarded as an opportunity to build for the future. Just as we often learn a lot from getting things wrong, we can indeed learn yet more from occasions where we feel *wronged*.

13. **Ask yourself: Perhaps this dream just wasn't meant to come true?** When we're disappointed, it's dangerously easy to see only the positive aspects of what it would have been like if we'd got our way. We're quite blind to all the things that might have gone wrong if our dream had come true. Some such dreams could have turned out to be nightmares.

14. **Remind yourself that you're still the same person.** You haven't suddenly become a lesser person. You might indeed *feel* like a lesser person, in that you're a mortified person – perhaps a justifiably mortified person. You may not have had an opportunity you wanted to be something different, or to do something different or to have something different, but you're still you. When you've come to terms with your disappointment – managed it – you will be a stronger person. Sadder perhaps, but more robust, more experienced, more

understanding of other people's disappointments, and better able to cope with your own next disappointment. The next set of suggestions aims to provide some positive actions you can do on your way to recovery.

Recovering from a Disappointment

In the previous set of tips we looked at the first steps involved in coming to terms with a disappointment. Next we explore some of the things you can do to climb back out of it.

1. **Re-examine your expectations.** Sometimes we expect too much – of ourselves, of other people, of both. Were your expectations inappropriate, or unfeasible, or unrealistic in the first place? If so, your disappointment is at least partly the result of something that you allowed to happen.

2. **Talk out your disappointment – and what you've learned from it.** This is one of the best ways of getting it out of your system and letting it go, while still building on what it's taught you. The ideal person to talk to in this context is someone who is good at listening, and will question you about your feelings and your plans to minimize similar disappointments in future, and who will help you to clarify your own thinking. Don't just be content with someone who merely offers advice.

3. **Don't outstay people's sympathy.** You may well have people around you who are sympathetic and understanding, and join in your grief for whatever it was you wanted but have been denied. Such sympathy can indeed be consoling – for a while. But sooner or later, *other people* will regard your disappointment as over and done with, and they won't continue to be sympathetic indefinitely.

4. **Be sensible about the time-scale of your disappointment.** Even if you felt humiliated, not many other people will still be thinking twice about it a week later. Probably no one will remember it a month later. The danger is that *you* could continue to dwell on it, long after anyone else has forgotten about it. You won't be doing yourself any good continuing to revisit the hurt.

5. **Lick your wounds, and get on with things.** Plan now for next time. After a damaging disappointment, you may not be ready to go 'full steam ahead' yet. But you can start moving again. This is the time to be realistic – no day-dreams, no brain surgery, no impossible targets. Work out what advice you can offer yourself for similar situations in future. Gradually, as you move ahead, the disappointment will be left further behind. It will gradually fade. It may never completely disappear, but it will become less and less significant to you.

6. **Acknowledge any weaknesses.** These are part of your learning from the disappointment. Look at each weakness as an (as yet) underdeveloped competence. Once acknowledged, plan to side-step any weaknesses so that they become less significant. Look around you at what other people do about the same sorts of weaknesses.

7. **What could you have done differently?** Sometimes that will be very clear, and the learning pay-off associated with the disappointment will be fairly straightforward to pin down. If, however, there was nothing you could have done differently, perhaps the disappointment was more to do with having had unjustified starry-eyed optimism, and the learning pay-off is about getting better at keeping your feet on the ground in future?

8. **Build on the experience.** All experience has at least some value, even if it's only to help us to get to know ourselves better. 'Sadder and wiser' are words offering little comfort but a lot of realism. We can only become wiser by learning from each experience of disappointment, and planning how to reduce the risk of repeating it next time round. The experience we gain helps us to *manage* ourselves more effectively, including those future times when we just aren't going to get what we think we want.

Overcoming Problems

However well we plan our lives, we are all faced with problems to overcome now and then. There are all sorts of problems: personal ones, study ones, 'people' ones, financial ones – you name it! The following suggestions can help you not only to work out how best to tackle various problems, but also to turn at least some of the problems to your advantage – there's useful learning pay-off to be gained by tackling and solving many of our problems.

1. **Accept that it's OK to have problems, at least sometimes.** Some would say that we're not really alive unless we've got some problems to tackle. We'd all prefer not to have any problems at all, but human nature is such that when we've not got any big problems, we seem to find ourselves some smaller ones to fuss over.

2. **Rationalize the meaning of 'problem'.** It's only really a problem when you've got no idea how to go about solving it. Once you know what you're going to do about it, a problem simply becomes a task to tackle.

3. **Admit when you may have a problem.** Sometimes a bigger problem is simply not facing up to when we have an actual problem to address. Hiding from problems doesn't make them disappear – and may indeed give them time to become more significant.

4. **Don't expect to have invented a brand-new unique problem.** Few people invent these! Most problems have been

experienced before, and will happen again to other people. This means that there will be other people around somewhere who know how they got over similar problems, and you yourself may be able to help other people to solve similar problems later too.

5. **Don't expect a 'quick fix' every time.** Some problems do lend themselves to ready-made rapid solutions, but others don't. Miracles sometimes happen, but don't wait in hope for one. Waiting in hope for a miracle can be time lost in finding a logical way to tackle a problem.

6. **Don't waste your time and energy allocating the blame for a problem.** Often, it's not your fault, but finding out who to blame doesn't make the problem go away. Sometimes it is your fault, but again there's no mileage in blaming yourself other than simply acknowledging what not to do another time.

7. **Work out who actually *owns* the problem.** That's not necessarily the same as working out whose fault it may be. Many people spend a lot of time worrying about problems that belong to other people, and there's not normally a lot that any of us can do about other people's problems. The only problems that you can really solve are those which belong to you, so it's worth checking this out at an early stage. You can of course *help* other people to go about solving their problems, and other people can likewise help you to solve yours – if you make this easy for them to do, rather than fighting them every step of the way.

8. **Pinpoint your problem.** When under a bit of pressure, it's all too easy to feel that the whole world is conspiring against you to make your life difficult. This is always just a feeling, and not a reality. Once you start being objective about your problems, it usually turns out that only a few things are getting you down, and sometimes it all boils down to just one real problem and a few other nuisances.

9. **Rank your problems in order of importance.** This is especially useful if you've got a number of problems on your mind. It can be quite a relief to work out which are the really important problems to tackle, and which can safely be relegated for later attention.

10. **Rank your problems again, this time in order of urgency.** Sometimes a small urgent problem can be more worthy of your attention than a larger, non-urgent problem. Getting a wise balance between urgent and important can save a lot of time and sweat in the long run.

11. **Think of problems one by one.** It's usually best to work systematically at solving one particular problem rather than trying to tackle them all at once. Knowing which are really important and which are urgent helps you to decide where to start solving your problems.

12. **Sometimes it helps to solve one or two little, easy problems first, before tackling the big important one.** This can help you to feel that you're at least making some headway, and get you into your stride for tackling the big one.

13. **Talk about a big problem to someone.** Talk to several different people if you can. Just putting your problem into words when explaining it to people often makes it seem less serious and more manageable. Choose carefully whom you wish to bring into your confidence. For some problems, it's useful to talk to someone you don't know well – even someone you may never want to talk to again once you're over the problem. Sometimes it's wise not to colour an important friendship with a particular problem.

14. **Work out why the problem arose in the first place.** This may not directly help you to solve it, but can help you to avoid similar problems arising in future. Finding the cause can often help you to plan how to go about solving a problem.

15. **Work out how you could make the problem worse!** Don't actually make it worse, of course. Actions that can solve the problem are quite often the reverse of the tactics that would have made it worse. Besides, thinking about how bad it could have become helps you to feel better about it not being so bad in reality.

16. **Decide _three_ ways you can improve the situation.** Think of something you can do straight away, something else to do very soon afterwards, and one longer-term action that will help to solve the problem.

17. **Tell someone what you're planning to do.** Especially when you're going to be tackling something difficult, it helps

when other people know what you're trying to achieve. They can help you to make sure that you do indeed try to do something about the problem straight away, rather than continue to postpone getting started on it.

18. **Keep a log of what you do.** This helps you to see that you're tackling the problem in a structured, organized way, and making progress, even when progress is slow.

19. **Regard each real problem as an opportunity to grow.** Even the most painful problem can turn out later to have been a valuable learning experience, equipping you with skills for the rest of your life. Not least, problems can help you to develop persistence, patience, confidence and determination.

Getting out of Trouble!

This set of tips is mostly about *staying* out of trouble, with some advice about getting out of it if you find yourself in it. Sadly, there are parts of the world that at times are not civilized, friendly and safe, and such a place at such a time may be just round your corner. Like many other parts of this book, we're only really thinking of common sense here, but sometimes wisdom comes with experience, and the wisest choice is to pre-empt bad experiences in the first place.

1. **Be aware that students sometimes get picked upon!** This can particularly happen when there are tensions – for whatever reason – between a student community and the local population. Such tensions may have genuine causes, such as the additional noise, litter and congestion that are caused by a significant influx of temporary residents.

2. **Minimize the chances that you'll be picked upon.** Any risk tends to be increased if it's late at night, if you're on your own, if there aren't many other people around, and if it's known to be a trouble-spot in the first place. Ask around to find out where *not* to be on your own, and when the danger times happen to be.

3. **Few things generate higher hostility than inappropriate parking!** If you've not got a car, of course, this isn't one of your worries – except if you're with a friend who gets into parking bother. But if you do have a car, remember it's a target as well as you, if feelings run high. Sometimes,

permanent residents resent anyone parking in what they feel
is *their* territory – even if legally they have no claim on it at all.
If challenged about parking, it's usually safest to comply and
move without protest. Even if you had a right to park there,
it's better not to risk damage or injury!

4. **Choose where and when you use cash machines.**
   Obviously, machines in dark places when there's no one
   around (except someone watching with intentions on your
   wealth) are not a good idea. Even in well-populated places, it's
   not a good idea to use a cash machine when you've got your
   hands full of shopping.

5. **Try not to be robbed.** No one *wants* to be robbed, but some
   make it easy for would-be robbers. For example, if you leave
   your credit card in the pocket of a jacket on a seat in a busy
   pub while you go to the bar to get in a round, don't be too
   surprised if it's gone next time you look for it.

6. **'Your money or your life!'** If you are confronted by this
   dreadful choice, the sensible approach is to hang on to your
   life. Better still, try to hang on to at least some of your money
   too, but at the cost of *appearing* to give in and hand over all of
   your worldly goods. Don't put all of your eggs in one pocket,
   or wallet or handbag – too easy for the poachers!

7. **Be quietly polite and co-operative when stopped by the
   police!** Sooner or later, you're likely to be stopped and
   questioned. The likelihood increases if you're out and about
   late (like many a student), and look young enough and fit
   enough to have done something wrong. Don't make a big
   deal of your rights. Answer their questions honestly and
   calmly. It's certainly not a good idea to make up a name and
   address! But whatever else you do . . .

8. **Admit nothing!** It's surprisingly easy to appear to be
   admitting something, particularly if you're a bit confused
   anyway, perhaps due to alcohol, or simply as a result of the
   surprise at being stopped and questioned. If you're believed to
   have admitted something, it's surprisingly difficult to 'un-
   admit' it afterwards.

9. **Continue to be co-operative if taken down to the police
   station!** Do continue to gently insist on your right to one
   telephone call. Think hard about who's going to be in the

best position to come to your rescue or vouch for you –
someone who will be there to take the call *now* is the best
person, not someone who will be there next morning
sometime. It's not a bad idea to always have a suitable
telephone number on your person.

10. **If you *have* done something wrong, and get caught, get
help.** You'll almost certainly not be the first person to have
got into trouble. Minimize the danger you're in by getting
someone with professional experience to help you towards
whatever course of action will be most appropriate for you. An
experienced student counsellor is trained to listen, advise, and
not judge.

11. **Be identifiable.** No one likes to think about the need to be
identifiable if they get knocked down by a bus, or if they pass
out on the street. But it's in your interest that your next of kin
(or someone else appropriate) can be reached in an
emergency. It could save your life, especially if there are
medical history circumstances to take into account.

12. **Keep a shortlist of useful addresses.** You never know
when you might need to contact key people at short notice.
This clearly applies to relatives and close friends, but also to
key contacts at college (perhaps head of department, personal
tutor, and so on). Back up this resource. If your address book
or diary or filofax gets lost, it could take forever building up
such details again. Include phone numbers, email addresses
and important postal ones.

Part VI

Revision – Getting Your Act Together

What Will Your Exams Really Measure?

This isn't so much a set of tips about exams (plenty of these coming later), but some food for thought to help you to get off to a good start in putting exams into perspective. In particular, we're thinking about the most common sorts of exam you're likely to meet – in a silent exam room, against the clock, answering questions you have only just seen when you sat down at your desk, with a pen in your hand, and a blank exam booklet into which you're to write your answers. The technical name for such exams is 'unseen, time-constrained written examinations'. (There are, indeed, other types of exam, for example open-book exams, 'seen' written exams, and multiple-choice exams, and separate sets of tips on these are included later in this book, but for now let's stay with the most common kind of exam.) You've had many such exams before. But have you ever stopped to think, calmly and logically, what's actually being measured when you do such exams? Now's your time to do so. However well – or badly – you've done in exams in the past, let's leave those behind and look ahead now. Let's look towards your *next* set of exams, and think of what will be measured then. Will it be:

1. **How much you know about your subject?** Written exams only measure this to a limited extent. After all, there will be countless things that you *do* know which don't happen to be asked for in the particular questions on the paper on that particular day. There will be things that you know which aren't relevant to the questions. We could say that written exams measure what you know about what the questions

actually ask for – a narrower cross-section of the total amount you know.

2. **How much you *don't* know about your subject?** Exams tend to measure how much you don't know about the particular questions you happen to answer. That's only part of what you don't know about your subject. But every time you don't know something that you need to answer a question well, you're missing out on marks you would have gained if you had known it.

3. **The quantity of revision you have done?** Exams don't really measure this. Clearly, if you've spent a great deal of time revising, you're likely to be better placed to do well in exams than if you only did a little revision. But *quality* of revision is much more important; see below.

4. **The quality of revision you have done?** Yes, exams measure this surprisingly well. If your revision has really focused on becoming skilled at answering questions, when you come to do so in exams you're at an advantage. Furthermore, if your revision has focused on you becoming *faster* at answering questions, you're even better placed, as you will have plenty of time to make your answers really good. The tips about revision processes in this book aim to help you maximize the quality of your revision – and that also means you don't necessarily have to spend so long doing it – good news!

5. **How intelligent you are?** Surely not. Intelligence means many different things, and can't be measured by any single method – not least exams. Exams may, however, measure how intelligently you approached your revision, and this book should help you bring your intelligence to bear on this.

6. **How much studying you have done just before the exams?** Not really. If you do *too much* studying right at the last minute you may well know a lot at the moment you sit down in the exam room, but you could be too *tired* to answer the questions well. In other words, you won't do yourself justice if you leave it all to last-minute revision.

7. **How well you keep your cool in the exams themselves?** Yes, exams do measure this. If you're calm and composed, you're in a much better state to read the questions carefully, and to think logically about what the questions are intended

to draw out from you, and to fine-tune your answers to get as many marks as possible for each question. So it's worth becoming better able to keep your cool in exams. But that in turn depends quite a lot on increasing your confidence. And that depends on *knowing* that you've prepared for the exams in a sensible and efficient way – and that brings us back again to the *quality* of your revision.

8. **How good your memory is?** Sadly perhaps, most written exams do indeed require some memory skills. There are things you need to know to pass exams. But what sort of 'knowing'? There are at least three sorts – 'know what', 'know how' and 'know why'. Some of this is about memory, but 'know how' in particular is about practice. That's why some of the most important suggestions in this book are about getting *practising* when you revise, and most importantly the idea of making yourself your own question bank so that you have something real to practise with.

9. **How good you have become at question spotting?** Most 'unseen' exams measure this to some extent. When you've correctly guessed some of the questions in advance, and practised answering them until you've become *good* at answering them, it's not surprising that you'll do better than otherwise. But there's a risk with question spotting. What if none of the questions you prepared for come up, and all the questions are about different aspects? That's where making a question bank of your own comes up trumps, because a good question bank will cover *all* of the questions which could possibly come up in your exam, not just the most obvious or likely ones.

10. **How fast you think?** Some kinds of exam measure how fast you think, for example multiple-choice computer-based exams, where you're not spending time writing things down, but making decisions and then selecting options. But written exams aren't so much about thinking fast as thinking *well*. And you don't actually get marks for what you think, only for what you *write* about what you think. And sometimes you'll think for a few seconds, but it takes you a minute or two to write down your thoughts. So don't be too concerned about quick thinking in the context of written exam technique.

11. **How fast you read the questions?** No! Written exams measure how *well* you read the questions, not how fast you read them. If you read them too fast, you're less likely to read them properly – you may miss the point of the questions. It's understandable in the heat of the moment to want to rush ahead and find out what the questions are all about, but you need to resist this temptation in exams. It's much more important to make sure that you know exactly what each question is asking you to do.

12. **How wisely you pick the questions that you answer?** Yes, this counts in many exams. Where you have a choice of questions, it is important that you pick the right ones – the ones where you're going to be able to give your best answers. You can only pick the right ones if you've read *all* of them slowly enough and carefully enough to be able to make informed decisions about which questions to go for. Even with the best of intentions, however, sometimes you'll get this wrong. This means you'll have wasted some time finding out that a particular question *wasn't* a good one for you, and will need to start another one. But it's useful to minimize the number of times this happens to you in future.

13. **How *often* you reread the questions?** Yes, exams do measure this. It's a really good habit to get into to reread the question you're answering every few minutes. This helps to make sure that you stick closely to the question in your answer, rather than wasting valuable time and energy writing down all sorts of other irrelevant stuff – there are no marks at all for things the questions *don't* ask for!

14. **How fast you write down your answers?** Sadly, yes, exams *do* measure to some extent how fast people write. If you're a fast writer, and a *legible* fast writer, this aspect of exams won't worry you. But if your writing is slower, you will need to take steps to compensate for this; you'll need to focus on the quality of what you write, rather than the quantity. This means fine-tuning your revision so that you *practise* composing short-but-good answers to questions.

15. **How legible your handwriting is?** Again, yes, written exams do measure this to some extent. Put it this way, if your examiners can't read your writing, they won't be able to give

you any marks! If they can only read it with difficulty, they won't be likely to give you as many marks as they would have done if they had been able to read it without any problem. So if your handwriting is bad when under time pressure, as in an exam, you may need to work at writing more slowly, and improving the quality both of your handwriting, and of what you say in your answers to questions.

16. **How well you set out your answers?** Sometimes this is important. Human nature being what it is, any examiner is likely to give slightly higher marks to a well set-out answer than to the same answer badly set out. There's more about this later in this book in the tips on writing exam answers.

17. **How well you manage your time** *during* **the exams?** Most exams measure this very well indeed! In time-constrained exams, you're working against the clock. So is everyone else. If you're better at this than other people, you score higher marks. So it's worth cultivating your time management in the exam room. There's a lot more advice about this later in this book.

18. **How carefully you** *read* **and** *edit* **your answers before handing in your script at the end of the exam?** Yes, this counts a lot too. You can almost always increase your mark very significantly by doing this. But this also means that you need to plan *time* to read your answers towards the end of each exam. And you need to be able to make useful additions and corrections as you read what you've written. There's detailed advice on how to go about this later in this book.

Making Your Own Question Bank

Imagine how pleased you'd feel if you could have a list, weeks in advance, of all the possible exam questions you needed to be able to answer. You can have exactly this! You can *make* just such a list for yourself. Making – and *using* – such a list of questions can be the key to effective, efficient revision. This in turn leads to good exam results, and everything that follows on from that. But what's a 'question bank' and how can you make one? The following tips explain more.

1. **If you know all of the questions, you're well on the way to being able to give all of the answers.** A common lament after exams is, 'If only I'd known what the questions were going to be. . . .' But you *can* work out what they could be, especially if you start collecting questions early.

2. **It's never too early to start collecting questions.** You can, in fact, start making a question bank as soon as you start studying something. You can even start writing down questions *before* you've done anything else – for example all the questions you can think of that, sooner or later, you suspect you may need to become able to answer.

3. **It's a useful habit to adopt.** Many students who've once been through the process of making and then using a question bank as an integral part of their studies continue to make such a bank a chosen study strategy. They often report that they find it one of the most efficient and effective methods of 'keeping tabs on' how their learning is going on a

day-to-day basis through a course. They also report that using a question bank as a revision tool is one of the best ways of ensuring that revision is focused and efficient.

4. **It's never too late to add further questions.** Even during the final stages of revising for an exam, you will often think of yet more questions you need to be able to answer. It's best, however, not to add *too* many questions at this late stage, or you may become discouraged by the amount that you still don't know about the topic.

5. **What sort of questions?** The questions that are most useful as part of your question bank are the short, sharp ones. Most of these questions will be one-liners (sometimes containing only a few words each). They all need to end with a question mark (to help you to practise answering them in due course), and all need to contain at least one *question* word or phrase.

6. **Keep asking yourself: 'What am I *reasonably* expected to become able to do with this?'** Ask yourself this question all the time – in lectures, when you're reading, when you're talking to other people, when you're thinking about a topic, and so on. Capture your thinking about what you could

reasonably be asked to do, then turn your thinking into
questions which you can aim to become able to answer.

7. **What's a question word or phrase?** These almost all have a
    word containing 'w' in them. Such words and phrases include
    'Why . . .?', 'What . . .?', 'Where . . .?', 'Who . . .?', 'How . . .?',
    'When . . .?'

8. **The word 'else' can be really useful in your question-
    bank questions.** For example, if you could already answer
    the questions 'Why . . .?', 'What . . .?', 'Where . . .?', 'Who . . .?',
    'How . . .?', 'When . . .?' about something, think how much
    more you'd know about it if you could *also* answer the
    following questions about the same thing: 'Why *else* . . .?',
    'What *else* . . .?', 'Where *else* . . .?', 'Who *else* . . .?', 'How
    else . . .?', 'When *else* . . .?'

9. **Use your syllabus.** In course handbooks or elsewhere, your
    syllabus will often be expressed in terms of 'intended learning
    outcomes', explaining in some detail what you will be
    expected to be able to do in due course to *show* that you've
    mastered each topic. It is often very useful to start with such
    learning outcomes, and turn them into a list of questions,
    which you can then systematically set about becoming able to
    answer effectively.

10. **The 'instruction' words from exam questions are useful
    too.** Just about all exam questions contain words or phrases
    such as 'Discuss . . .', 'Describe . . .', 'Explain . . .', 'Show
    that . . .', 'Prove that . . .', 'Compare . . .', 'Contrast . . .',
    'Compare and contrast . . .', 'Evaluate . . .', 'Distinguish
    between . . .', 'Summarize . . .', 'List five reasons why . . .',
    'Decide . . .', and so on.

11. **How many short questions make a question bank?** The
    more the better. Question banks can contain hundreds of
    short questions – even thousands. If you can answer all of
    these short questions, you can automatically answer any longer
    question. Even the most complex exam question is only a lot
    of short questions rolled into one.

12. **Use your lectures to get questions for your question
    bank.** During a lecture, every time you sense that something
    is really important, turn it there and then into a question for
    your question bank. Don't wait till hours later to do this – the

questions may have evaporated from your mind by then.
Capture them during the lecture. Write them into your notes,
or directly into a question bank that you have already started
and have there with you.

13. **Add worked examples done in lectures or tutorials.**
Often, lecturers use worked examples to illustrate the kinds of
question you need to become able to answer under your own
steam in due course. Lecturers sometimes adapt such
questions for forthcoming exams, perhaps changing them just
a little for that purpose.

14. **Keep questions and answers apart.** When you've got
worked examples or solved problems in your lecture notes, it's
useful to write the *question* itself into your question bank, so
that you can look at it again, *without* the answer directly in
sight. This gives you the chance to have another go at the
question on your own from scratch, without the temptation
just to read the answer you've already got. It can be useful to
include a note to remind you of where the answer can be
found, so that you can look it up quickly (but not *too* quickly!)
if you have trouble trying to answer the question on your own
as you revise.

15. **Add any questions or tasks set as homework or
suggested follow-up work.** Once again, keep the questions
apart from the work you may have done yourself on them, so
that you remain able to practise on the questions without
risking 'cheating yourself' by looking too soon at the answers.

16. **When you read books, handouts, articles, web pages,
etc., continue to gather questions.** For example, if you're
reading a particular paragraph, ask yourself, 'What question is
this paragraph the answer to?' If it turns out to be an
important question – one that *you* may need to be able to
answer – capture the question, and add it to your question
bank.

17. **Trawl textbooks and other source material for worked –
or open – questions.** Most source materials contain both
worked examples and further questions for students to try,
sometimes indeed with answers in an appendix. When you
find questions that are directly relevant to your own syllabus, it
can be useful to copy selected questions into your question

bank, along with notes to prompt you about the source of the question, and where you can find the solution or answer if it is available.

18. **Use old exam papers to fine-tune your question bank.** A big advantage of doing this is that it helps you to find out the expected *standard* of the questions you need to prepare in order to be able to answer yourself. It helps you to see *how many* short, sharp questions are involved in a typical exam question.

19. **Do some question spotting.** It's always useful to put your mind to what may be due to come up as an exam question. You could be spot-on, and thus have the opportunity to practise so that you will be able to answer such a question easily, quickly and painlessly – it's worth the chance! Even when the questions you think of don't come up, at least some of the knowledge you've gained by practising with them is likely to be useful in answering the questions that do come up.

20. **Capture other people's questions too.** For example, if in a lecture someone else asks a question, jot that question down yourself – you too may need to be able to answer that question in due course.

21. **Build your question bank with like-minded fellow-students.** If you build a question bank along with several friends, you'll all end up with a much better question bank than any of you could have built up individually. You'll each tend to think of at least some questions that no one else thought of.

22. **Don't worry yet about being able to *answer* all of your questions.** The important thing is that you've captured the questions themselves. Once you've captured a question, it's relatively straightforward to find out what the answer might be. You can look it up, or ask fellow-students, or ask a lecturer – or work it out for yourself sometimes.

Using Your Question Bank

In the previous set of tips, we looked at the purpose of making a question bank, and at a variety of ways of gathering questions for it. Next, we'll look at some ways of turning it into a really useful learning tool, and at processes for putting it to work to help you master your subject material.

1. **Consider making it a portable tool.** For example, if you get yourself a pocket-sized notebook, you could use different parts of the book to write in questions for different subjects, with index tabs to help you find each topic easily. 'Post-its' can be inserted instead of index tabs.
2. **Think about numbering the questions for each topic.** This gives you a way of keeping track more easily of which questions you *can* answer without any difficulty, and which are going to need a bit more practice or research before you get them firmly into your repertoire.
3. **Explore whether it will be helpful for you to have both questions and prompts in your question bank.** If you do decide to do this, however, it's best to keep the prompts out of sight of the questions. For example, if one page had 17 short, sharp questions as a numbered list, you could write overleaf a set of prompts also numbered 1–17. These should be just enough to *start* you off towards answering the question, for those occasions where the answer has 'slipped'. Sometimes, however, if the answer to the question is very short, you might prefer to simply include it in your prompts –

for example if the question involved a calculation, you could use the right answer as your prompt.

4. **Would you be happier making an electronic question bank?** If you happen to have easy access to the sort of software used for making multiple-choice tests, for example, you could build up your own question bank as a computer-aided learning programme. Your 'prompts' could be summoned up on-screen by pressing a 'help' button. The only problem with making a computer-based question bank is that you could be limited in the places you could use to practise with it; you'd need to be at your machine – or any machine if you put your question bank on floppy disk or CD, for example.

5. **Some students prefer playing cards.** You could, alternatively, write a few questions on filing cards – the sort you may well be using for keeping track of your literature searching. You could write the question on one side of the card, and a prompt on the other side. You could file the cards in a box, with index cards separating one subject from another. You could then draw a card from your box at random, and see how well you were able to answer the question on it.

6. **Don't just make it, *use* it.** Like any other tool, a learning tool such as a question bank only does a useful job if you put it to work. Your aim should be to continue practising answering your questions, until you become able to do so easily and correctly.

7. **Regard it as good news every time you find a question you can't yet answer.** It's always useful to find out something now which you didn't know you didn't yet know. This is far better than only finding it out when it's too late to do anything about it.

8. **Find out more about those questions you can't answer *repeatedly*.** These are the ones that are going to need your attention. They are usually the most difficult questions. However, the more often you *fail* to answer a question, then try to find out how to answer it, the less likely you are to forget it yet again. It's often the questions on which you practised several times that turn out to be the most valuable ones in your question bank.

9. **Don't waste much time on the questions you can answer easily.** While it's always very pleasant to sit there answering straightforward questions successfully, you're not learning as much doing this as you would struggling a little harder with the questions which are more difficult or where the answers seem elusive.

10. **Check, however, that you *can* answer those questions which you think you've mastered.** Being able to answer what seems like an easy question is something you shouldn't take for granted until you've *done it* at least once. It's quite possible to sit there thinking, 'Yes, I know how to do this', but not yet actually be able to do it.

11. **Turn it into a game.** If you've got your questions on cards in a box, you can draw cards at random to help you ring the changes between one subject and another. You could 'file' the cards bearing questions you had no difficulty with in one box, and those cards bearing questions needing attention in another box. You could then come back to these on another day, and give them that extra practice they need.

Putting Revision into Perspective

If you're heading for important exams, there's no getting round the fact that revision is one of the most important things you'll do as a student. Few people do well in exams without doing some serious revision first. The following tips should help you to adjust your priorities to make sure that revision happens.

1. **Remind yourself what's in it for you.** Doing revision well involves some hard work, but it's in your own best interests. There's nothing worse than later in your life looking back and wishing you'd put more time and energy into your revision, so that you'd have got a better qualification, and a better job, and a better house, and a better car, and so on! You're investing in your own future when you revise. At the end of the day, you're doing it for *you* and no one else (even if you do have people around you nagging you to put your back into it – parents, tutors, partner, friends and so on).

2. **Get past 'If only I'd started revision months ago!'** There's a whole set of tips coming up soon to help you get rid of any 'revision-avoidance strategies' you might own. If you *did* start revision in really good time, you can justifiably feel rather smug reading these tips. However, not many people feel that they started early enough – even if they have been revising long before exams loom up. So now isn't the time for 'If only I'd started . . .'. What you've got left is the time between now and your exams. Your most important business is using this time well.

3. **Quality counts, not just quantity.** As you'll see when you continue working through the tips on revision, there's a lot you can do to make it more efficient and effective. Beware of feeling that if you're doing long hours of revision, it must be good enough. Concentrate on the learning pay-off you're gaining from your revision, not just the hours spent.

4. **Decide that revision isn't just 're-vision'!** High-quality revision is actually a lot more than simply 'having another look' at what you've already been through. There are many topics where it will take a lot more than just 'seeing it again' for you to feel you are confident in tackling them.

5. **Revision is about building your confidence.** When you know something well, and you *know* that you know it well, your confidence increases. In turn, the more confident you become, the more successful you will be when you put into practice that which you have revised – for example when you use your gained knowledge to answer exam questions.

6. **Don't spend ages doing low-level things instead of getting started with your revision.** Because revision feels like a big, daunting task, it's all too easy to put off the evil moment of actually starting it for days, weeks or months! You'll have all manner of revision-avoidance tactics to choose from – but you'll feel much better if you resist these, and get stuck in. That probably means *now*.

7. **Practice makes perfect.** This is particularly true of revision for exams. What you really need to be doing is practising for the exam. That in turn means practising answering questions, practising solving problems, practising whatever you'll be asked to do in the exam room.

8. **Revision involves a set of transferable skills.** This won't be the last time in your life you need to get your head round a range of subject material in preparation for working with it in an assessed context (for example, writing your answers to exam questions). From time to time in just about any career, you'll find yourself in a similar situation, where you need to absorb a substantial amount of new material, and then *show* that you've done so by putting it all to work in some way. Therefore it's worth becoming *really good* at the whole business of revising.

9. **Remind yourself about what exams really measure.** It
    could be worth going back to the very first part of this section
    of the book, and checking once more the various things that
    are measured by typical against-the-clock exams. In particular,
    check which of these things are your own personal danger
    spots – whether it is to do with speed of writing, reading the
    questions too quickly, picking the wrong questions, or not
    leaving yourself time to make adjustments at the end of the
    exam. Make a checklist of your own danger areas. Keep your
    own personal checklist in mind as you work through the tips
    which follow, so that your chosen revision tactics match up
    well to your own particular needs.

10. **Fine-tune your revision to prepare for the particular
    kinds of exams you're heading towards.** Most of the tips
    on revision and exams in this book are about the most
    common kind of exam (i.e. time-constrained unseen written
    exams) where you're working against the clock, and don't
    know what the questions are going to be until you see them in
    the exam room. However, there are different kinds of exam,
    for example open-book exams, 'seen' written exams (where
    you *do* know what the questions are going to be) and multiple-
    choice exams. There are separate sets of tips for these sorts of
    exam later in this book.

Planning Your Revision Timetable

Since revision is a really important task, it's worth investing at least some planning into the overall way you tackle it. Equally, however, you need to be careful not to spend all of your time planning it, and then not leave yourself enough time or energy to actually get round to *doing* it. The following tips will help you to strike a sensible balance between planning and action.

1. **Make yourself a chart for your revision timetable.** The advantage of having it all on one sheet of paper (a large one if you have one) is that you can stick it up on a wall, where it will be a reminder to you. It is also reassuring to be able to tick off topics and subjects as you work through your plan, so that you know how your overall progress is going.
2. **Don't plan too firmly.** If your revision timetable is too rigid, you'll soon abandon it! It's much better to make your timetable reasonably flexible, so that you can make adjustments to it as often as you need to. For example, sometimes it will take you less time than you expected to revise a topic, and you can then slip some other topics into the time you've saved yourself. Equally, some things will take longer than you expected, and you'll need to be able to find the extra time you need for them.
3. **Don't plan to revise for every minute of every day.** Life has to go on while you're revising. That includes eating,

sleeping, relaxing, socializing, and simply being a human being. At most, plan two or three hours of revision for each day when you're fitting revision around other activities such as going to classes, writing up coursework, and so on. Even when there's *nothing* left in your diary besides revision (for example the final weeks before your exams start), don't imagine your brain will agree to hard labour from first light to midnight – brains don't work that way!

4. **Plan some time off.** It's really important to have the odd day or half-day when part of your plan is *not* to do any revision at all. This helps you to get the most from such breaks. It's far better to be enjoying a *planned* break than to have slunk away from your revision load and absconded. You'll also find it easier to keep your revision productivity up, when you know it's not going to be too long before a planned break.

5. **Build variety into your plans.** For example, don't plan to revise topic A for days on end. It's much more efficient to do a short spell of topic A, then move on to topic B for an hour, then perhaps to topic C before going back and continuing with topic A. Here a change is *almost* as good as a rest.

6. **Plan to revise everything more than once.** Some things will need to go several times 'through your brain' for you to really master them. Revising something three times in one sitting is rarely as good as revising the same thing in three different sittings. Sometimes, you need to allow some time between revision episodes for your mind to continue working subconsciously.

7. **Overall, make your revision plan a humane one.** You need to be able to live comfortably with your plan. If the plan is too fearsome, it won't be surprising if you rebel against it, and drift off into unplanned revision or – worse – leave revision altogether.

8. **Consider making your plan 'public'.** For example, if you pin it up where other people can see it, they can remind you of your plan if you seem to be slipping from it. Also, it can help other people to realize that you won't be as available for normal socializing while you're revising. They can then help you to keep to your plans. Of course if the people around you are likely to mock you for being so intelligent and

conscientious as to have made a sensible plan, you may decide
not to share your plan with them.

9. **Think twice about trying to revise absolutely everything.**
You probably won't have time to revise everything on your
syllabus – at least, not to revise it all *really well.* When your
exams give you at least some degree of choice over which
questions you tackle, it can be better to have revised *most*
things in some depth, rather than everything at a superficial
level. Remember that you only get marks from the questions
you actually answer – you don't get any marks for all the
wonderful things you know which *aren't* part of your exam
questions agenda.

10. **Ring the changes with revision processes as well as with
topics.** If you're doing the same kind of thing for too long,
you'll get bored with it – and this reduces your efficiency.
There are several quite different things you can do, all of
which boil down to useful revision. The more of these you can
build into any one day, the greater will be your learning pay-
off, the better you will feel about your revision, the more
confident you will become, and the more successful you are
likely to be. It can be an upward spiral.

Getting Started with Your Revision

Remember 'work-avoidance strategies'? Most people have become experts at putting off starting revision! You've probably done this already, possibly frequently. Now's the time to exorcize those work-avoidance strategies. Below I've listed some of the most common 'reasons' that people put forward for *not* starting revision quite yet. Actually, as you'll see, they're none of them *reasons* for not starting revision yet – they're *excuses*. Which of these are *your* excuses?

1. **'I can't start revision yet – I've not yet got enough to start revising.'** Yes, you have! Even if you've just started a course or a module, you've already got enough to start making your question bank. And if you make a summary of the last two or three lectures or classes, you've already started revising them. That's already an investment in your success with those particular little bits of your syllabus.

2. **'I'm too busy with coursework at the moment; I'll start revising when the pressure eases off a bit.'** Another excuse, I'm afraid. Coursework – if you let it – will expand to fill up all of your available time. It can become a very comfortable (but false) reason not to make a start on revision. And even if the coursework counts for 50% of your final marks, the other 50% may be for exams – and that means revision. I suggest you *first* spend a little time on revision every time you set about doing some coursework, *then* get on with the coursework. You may get very slightly fewer marks for that coursework, but you'll be investing in your exam marks, steadily, purposefully and efficiently. That in turn will increase your confidence, and that will increase your exam marks!

3. **'If I learn it now, I'll just forget it all again.'** There is, of course, some truth in this. But it's actually *useful* to learn things and then forget them. This helps you to find out exactly *what* you're likely to forget next time round. And once you've learned something and then forgotten it, it takes you far less time to learn it again, and again. So gradually you need to spend less and less time catching up on the things you've forgotten.

4. **'I'm still getting new material – I'll wait till we've got through the syllabus.'** Yet another excuse. You may indeed continue to get new material almost right up till your exams. If you were to leave all of your revision until you'd stopped getting new material, there just wouldn't be time to do that revision at all. So start revising with what you've already got.

5. **'No one else seems to be revising yet – why should I?'** Perhaps it's not cool to be seen to be starting your revision early? Perhaps other people *are* indeed revising already, but just not letting on about it? But in any case, you're not going to gain or lose exam marks on the basis of the revision *other*

people do, it's your own revision which counts. Now's your chance to get ahead of your fellow-students, by making your own start on revising. There's no need to crow about it, if you feel that would damage your reputation.

6. **'I know I *should* start revising now, but I just can't face it.'** At least this is an honest excuse. But if it's one of your excuses, you're actually giving yourself a bad time by thinking this way. You may be squandering useful mental energy trying to justify *not* starting yet, and with the same amount of energy you could have made a start, and would feel much better about it all. It's your choice, of course, but you know what makes sense.

7. **'I need a life – I can't be revising all the time now.'** That is true, of course. But a sensible revision strategy takes into account the fact that you need time for relaxation, and builds around this. The earlier you start revising, the less damage revision will do to your lifestyle. If revision becomes a small but important part of most days, that's better than postponing it until it needs to become the whole of some days – and that doesn't actually work when those days come along. If you leave it all till later, you're just creating a time period where you won't have time for a normal life.

8. **'But it will make me anxious when I find things I can't understand.'** This too is an excuse, not a reason. One of the *purposes* of starting revision really early is to allow plenty of time for just such things. The sooner you know that a particular topic is going to prove difficult to learn, the better. And in practice, the anxiety of finding that something is difficult is a lot less wearing than the vague fear that things may be difficult.

9. **'I've always been able to do it at the last minute.'** Possibly true. But it is also possible that this time it's going to be different. In fact this is probable. This time round, you probably have a lot more that will need to be revised. The subject material is almost certainly harder and more complex. The exams may be more important. The standards may be higher. There are several unknowns here. Starting your revision early is your best insurance against each and every one of these unknowns.

10. **No more excuses left?** As you've seen above, most reasons
     people give for putting off starting revision turn out to be
     excuses. The best thing to do about revision is simply to get
     started. It doesn't have to be much. Even 5 minutes spent
     making a summary, or 10 minutes writing down 10 questions
     to practise on, is a start. But don't stop. Once started, it's best
     to do some revision just about every working day. You can
     even earn the pleasure of feeling really pleased with yourself if
     you squeeze in a few minutes' revision on your days off too.
     It's almost worth it, just for the satisfaction it brings.

Revision Processes

What works best? As we've already seen, a productive revision strategy includes a variety of processes. Some revision processes bring much higher learning pay-off than others. In the following set of tips, I've turned my suggestions into **do's** and **don'ts**. But first, and most important:

1. **Do some revision** *before* **everything else you do.** Just a few minutes will do, especially in the early days and weeks. However, if you're doing one or more 'few minutes' slots of revision most days, it doesn't take long to start to build up a very significant investment in revision achieved.

2. **Keep your learning pay-off meter turned on.** Probably the most important thing about revision is to keep checking that it's really working for you. If you find yourself sitting, turning the page every few minutes, but with absolutely nothing going on in your mind, you might as well be doing something else or sleeping. Check which revision processes really work for you, and how well you remember things you've revised using them. The tips below cover some processes you will know already, but perhaps also some you haven't tried yet.

3. **Revise in spurts, not slogs.** The trouble with 'slogs' is that you get bored, tired, and fed up, and aren't likely to return to revision very spontaneously. A short 'spurt' doesn't tire you out, and leaves you time to do everything else on your agenda. And there's always time for another spurt.

4. **Don't just read things over and over again.** Reading, on

its own, doesn't usually have much learning pay-off. Another danger with reading is that it can take far too long. It can take nearly as long to read the same thing for the tenth time as it took the first time round. You haven't got time to just read and read.

5. **Don't read without a pen in your hand.** If, for example, you're making summary notes very frequently while you read, you're keeping your brain much more active than if you were just reading. Better still, write down questions to add to your question bank, continuously, as you read. Then you'll end up with learning tools such as summaries and questions, and will have gained much more than just the material you've read.

6. **Don't write too many long essays.** It's worth writing *some* full answers as part of your revision strategy, but you haven't time to make this a central plank of your strategy. The benefit of writing an essay now and then is that you can keep an eye on your speed, and gain awareness of how much you will be likely to be able to do in (say) an hour of exam time. However, in the time you take to write one full essay, you could write half a dozen *essay plans*. Writing an essay plan can take you through perhaps 90% of the *thinking* that you would put into a whole essay. Therefore writing several essay plans can involve a great deal more learning pay-off per hour than writing one whole essay.

7. **Practise writing out answers to some past exam questions.** This is *real* practice towards doing the same in your forthcoming exams. You can try answering questions without looking things up in your source materials, or you can give yourself the luxury of tracking down important material from your sources when you need it – keeping an eye on how long it takes you to do so.

8. **Use marking schemes, if you can get your hands on them.** When lecturers set exams, they usually design a marking scheme to make it easier (and fairer) to mark candidates' answers. Sometimes you'll have opportunities to use marking schemes yourself – for example if you're given self-assessment exercises where you mark your own work, or peer-assessment exercises where you mark other students' work. It can be very useful to use (or invent for yourself)

marking schemes to apply to work you do as you practise to become able to answer exam questions well.

9. **Practise answering short sharp questions.** In other words, put your question bank to work. Use it as a learning tool. Find out which questions you *can* answer without difficulty, and feel good about these. Find out, moreover, which questions you *can't yet* answer without looking things up, and feel even better about these – you've latched on to them in time to do something about becoming able to answer them on demand.

10. **Sometimes practise *speaking out* the answers to your short sharp questions.** This takes less time and energy than writing them out – but still gives you just as much thinking to do. The act of speaking out an explanation can in itself sometimes help you to remember it for longer than if you'd just written it out.

11. **Keep making new summaries.** Summarizing is a process with high learning pay-off. You can't help but think deeply when you make yourself a summary of something – you're deciding what's important enough to include, and what's marginal enough to leave out. And when you've done it, you've got something to *show* for it – the summary you've made. That in itself is another useful learning tool for future use.

12. **Make summaries of your summaries!** Continue the process of boiling down what you really need to remember to smaller and smaller amounts. This makes the whole business of revision more manageable and less daunting. Return to your summaries frequently, and practise fleshing them out to regenerate the bigger picture from which you condensed them.

13. **Do it with a friend – or more.** Some revision activities really lend themselves to working with fellow-students who are preparing for the same exams. For example, if you quiz each other using your question banks, your revision will not only be more active, but it will be more fun! When someone fires a question at you, you tend to think harder than if you'd just fired it at yourself – and, more importantly, there will be someone judging how well you answer it, which means you'll try harder to answer it well.

14. **Go back now and then to things you have no problems with.** It's reassuring to remind yourself how much you already know, and how much you can already do on demand. It's also an insurance against losing the ground you've already gained.

15. **Keep going back to things you struggled with, but got right eventually.** These are the things that are likely to slip away again unless you invest in some practice with them. It takes less time every time you return to them. Something you've gone back to ten times will by then hardly take any time at all to refresh in your mind.

16. **Revise everywhere!** Always have something with you which you can use for some revision. But don't carry everything around with you! All you need, for example, is a small chunk of your question bank, or a couple of summaries. Wherever you are, spend a little time getting to grips with even just a tiny bit of the big picture of your revision.

17. **Use little bits of time – lots of them.** Don't wait until you have a good solid three unbroken hours coming up – you don't get many such spells of time in your life! Use a few minutes here, a few minutes there, and so on. Lots of short spells are in fact much better than a few long spells of revision. For a start, you're much more alert during the first few minutes of each spell. In a longer spell, you would gradually sink into a state of inefficiency – and indeed boredom – you probably know that all too well from your past experiences of revision.

18. **Stop for a break right in the middle of things!** This may seem like bad advice, but think about it. If you were to plod on till you reached a tidy logical stopping place, you'd probably forget a lot more than if you stop revising quite suddenly right in the thick of thinking about something. When you return after your break, you'll then find that your mind is still full of the thoughts you had before your break, and you quickly get back into the swing of it.

Some Final Tips on Last-minute Revision

By now, you should know that my advice regarding last-minute revision is 'Don't do it!' But it's actually quite difficult *not* to do any revision in the final few hours before an exam. So this next set of tips is about making sensible decisions about whether you'll do any last-minute revision or not, and, if you decide to do some, how best to approach it.

1. **Don't do any *serious* revision this late.** By now, you should have done most of your revision. If there's still a large chunk of material you haven't yet revised, you're unlikely to gain anything significant by tackling it during these final hours.
2. **Don't tire yourself out revising now.** Each and every mark you score in your exam will be for what you write into the exam booklet. If you end up tired because you did too much last-minute revision, you may indeed *know* more, but not be able to do the questions justice because you're simply too *tired* to answer them well. Save your energy for the exam itself.
3. **Don't try to learn anything new now.** If you can't settle and feel you still have to be doing something to prepare for the exam, concentrate on things you've already learned quite well. The problem with learning something new is that if it turns out to be difficult, it can depress you. 'How much *else* don't I know yet?', you could find yourself thinking. Not good for morale.
4. **Don't spend time on the hard bits now.** This too could be depressing. If you find you've forgotten something important

again you could start thinking 'How many *other* important things have I forgotten?' Bad for morale.

5. **Do a little gentle polishing.** Work with things you know well. Use your question banks, and remind yourself how well you know them. Try sketching out mind maps or summaries just to get the topics flowing smoothly through your mind once more.

6. **Don't go back to your original lecture notes, textbooks and sources.** Last-minute revision is the time to concentrate on the summaries you've made during the course of your revision. The problem with going back to original sources just before an exam is that with that extra adrenalin in your system, you tend to notice in them things you've never noticed before. 'How much *more* have I never noticed before?' leads to a downward spiral in morale.

7. **Spend a few minutes making a list of the topics you reckon you know really well.** This could help you make better choices when you see the questions. It's also good for your confidence levels to remind yourself of things you've mastered.

8. **Don't spend very long on any one thing.** Don't get your mind too full of any one thing at this stage. Do a little of this, then a little of that, and so on.

Part VII

Exams – Before, During and After!

Just Before an Exam

The next set of tips is about a range of things to do on the last few days before an exam, right up to the moment of walking into the exam room and taking your seat. Like the related tips on last-minute revision in the previous section, all of these suggestions are just common sense. But with your feelings running high, anxiety mounting, and everyone around you in a similar state, such common sense often gets forgotten. Now's your chance to take stock of what *you* will do next time just before an exam.

1. **Check the exam timetable carefully.** Some institutions put exam timetables up on notice-boards, showing when and where each exam will take place. There's often a *draft* timetable, then the *final* one. This is because there often have to be some changes of date and place because of conflicts between different modules, or rooms not being big enough for the number of candidates who will be attending. So make *very* sure that you do a careful check through the *final* timetable, and don't end up sleeping in your bed when one of the exams is taking place! There's always *someone* who does this; make sure it's not you.

2. **Find out where each exam will be.** Sometimes you'll already know the venue, if it's a room that has been used for your classes, or a main hall, or sports hall, and so on. But there could be a location you've not been to before; if so, go and find out exactly where it is. You don't want to be the

only person who can't find it on the day, and end up there hot and sweaty and anxious 10 minutes after the exam has started.

3. **Double-check times and places with fellow-students.** Talk to people who are taking the same exam, and make sure they've got the same time and venue as you have for it. This ensures that you haven't made the same mistake each time *you* looked at the exam timetable – and it may be helpful to them if they've got it wrong for any reason.

4. **Assemble your stuff early.** The day before an exam, get together the things you'll need for it – pens (at least one spare), pencils, drawing instruments, calculator (with new battery, of course), tissues, highlighter pen perhaps, Tippex perhaps, and anything else you need to take in with you. Put all of these things in one plastic folder or envelope or whatever, in a visible place, so that you just have *one* thing to find and take when you set off for the exam.

5. **Try to avoid stressful situations.** You've got extra adrenalin in your system. Now's not the time to have a row with your partner or flatmates or neighbours. Don't argue with anyone about anything. Don't let yourself get angry about anything. Don't let yourself get hurt by anything or anyone. Back off from trouble. Shrug things off.

6. **Set your alarms.** If it's an early-morning exam and there's any chance you'd sleep in, take that worry away by having back-up systems to make sure you're up and awake when you need to be. Don't sit up all night in case you don't wake up! Arrange alarm clocks, mobile phones, a friend to bang on your door at an agreed time, someone to ring you up to check you're in the land of the awake, and so on. Then you can relax all the more.

7. **Get some rest.** Better still, sleep. Sleeping is a good way of passing the night before an important exam. Sleeping helps your brain recover energy to use for the exam itself. You're doing yourself more good by sleeping than you would if you stayed up all night revising. But what if you can't sleep? Don't worry, just rest. This is just as good for you. Relax with some music (quietly if other people are sleeping). Think of something *not* on tomorrow's exam – something quite boring

– that usually helps towards sleep. Don't lie awake worrying about not being asleep.

8. **Aim to be there early.** Get an *earlier* bus or train than the one you'd normally get. Or allow time for an alternative if the car won't start. Allow for a search for a parking place. Allow for a traffic jam. Being late for an exam uses up a vast amount of mental energy – energy that you need for the exam itself. 'What if they won't let me in?' 'Will it be very embarrassing?' There's no harm getting there an hour early – as long as you do sensible things when you arrive. See below!

9. **Be aware of the consequences of being late for an exam.** Obviously, if you're late, you won't have as much time as everyone else to score marks, and you won't do as well as you would have done if you'd been on time. But they might not even let you in, if you're late. Many institutions have a policy that no one may be admitted after 30 minutes or so. This is often coupled with a policy that no candidate may leave the exam *before* 30 minutes or so have elapsed. This is to make sure that there is no chance of someone going in to find out what the questions are, then leaving and passing on this information to people who've arranged to come in late, with just enough time to get clued up on some important information that may help them to answer the questions!

10. **Keep away from all the other people taking your exam.** Do you remember that crowd outside an exam room before an exam? Imagine the conversation. 'Do *you* know anything about Sprocket's Theorem?' 'Can *you* make sense of Dr Jinks' notes?' 'Do you think we'll get a question on Bogey's Principle?' And so on. Every time your ears catch something you *don't* know, they prick up. Bit by bit, you come to the conclusion that everyone around you knows all about everything, and that you know nothing and might as well go away. Best not be in that crowd at all.

11. **Find somewhere you can wait calmly.** For example, if you go to a coffee machine in a different building, you may be well away from all that pre-exam chatter about *your* exam. There may be other anxious people there asking each other questions like 'Can *you* derive the Clausius–Clapeyron

Equation?' and so on, but this doesn't worry you at all as this isn't on *your* exam.

12. **Double-check that you have nothing incriminating on your person.** Cheating in exams is taken seriously – don't risk being accused of intending to cheat, because a folded-up summary of 'thermodynamics' fell out of your pocket onto the floor when you pulled out your handkerchief to sneeze! Don't even have someone's telephone number written on the back of your hand.

13. **Don't forget a loo stop.** Not many people forget such a thing before an exam – nature has a way of reminding us of such things when there's a bit of anxiety around. But it's worth making sure that you avoid any avoidable discomfort – for example in the later stages of a long exam. Few people do their greatest writing when needing to visit the loo. And of course, visiting the loo in the middle of an exam is not

straightforward – someone would have to make sure you hadn't hidden Smith and Jones's book in one of the cubicles, and so on!

14. **Keep thinking positive.** As the minutes till 'doors open' tick away, allow your mind to dwell on the things you *can* do. Shut out any thoughts about things you *can't* do. It's the things you *can* do which will be the basis of the marks you're about to score.

15. **Get some oxygen into your bloodstream.** No, I'm not suggesting a workout in the gym until the doors open. But walk around and breath in some air – outside if it's pleasant – within sight of the building your exam is in. Aim to be there just about when the doors are opening, and walk in and find your seat.

Those First Few Minutes

OK, you're now at your desk in the exam room. Probably your pulse rate is up a bit. Your palms may be a bit sweaty. Your breathing may be a bit faster and shallower. You may be feeling a little like a scared rabbit – but you *know* a lot more than most scared rabbits. Or, of course, you may be your normal cool self, completely in control. No matter which, the next few minutes are important. There's a lot you can do to make them pay dividends for you. Here goes.

1. **Get comfortable.** Exam rooms are rarely the most comfortable places in the world, but make the best of a bad job. Adjust your chair and get your feet planted as comfortably as you can. Move things around on your desk or table until your writing arm and hand are positioned as naturally as you can manage. Try to relax your neck and back, and take a few slow, deep breaths to get some oxygen into your bloodstream. It's the equivalent of limbering up for a sporting activity, but this time the focus is your brain.

2. **Check that you're looking at the *right* question paper.** Just a glance will tell you this. In large exam rooms, there are often several different exams going on at once; there could have been a mix-up, and you might be at the wrong desk. If so, best find this out straightaway and get it sorted out. It's not a good idea to spend the first half-hour doing someone else's exam – even if you know all about the subject.

3. **Don't start doing anything before you're given the go-ahead.** Some exam systems get everyone settled into their places and then someone says 'Start now, please.' In other places, you just go to your desk and get on with it. Glance around and see what everyone else is doing. Only *glance* now – don't stare – someone might think you are trying to communicate with other candidates. When it's OK to do so, get going as below.

4. **Do the 'admin' bits and pieces.** Systems vary, but you'll no doubt have your candidate number to write onto the exam booklet, the date, the exam topic, and somewhere you'll have to write your name, so that they know who you are, even if the name is on a slip of paper that is collected in quite separately soon after the exam has started. Doing these admin tasks helps you to settle down. However tense you may feel, it's unlikely that you won't remember you name. The date, if you need it, will probably be on the question paper anyway. It seems like an age sometimes, but this is the first half-minute or so gone.

5. **You're absolutely *dying* to see the questions, but don't look just yet!** First, check the instructions. They call it the 'rubric' – the bit which tells you how many questions to do, how long the exam is, whether you've got a completely free choice of questions, or whether you've got to do *one* from Section A then *two* from Section B. Find out whether all of the questions carry equal marks or not. Find out whether there's a compulsory question. You wouldn't believe how many candidates lose valuable marks just because they *didn't* read the instructions, and answered (for example) two questions from Section A, but only the *first* one (usually, according to Sod's Law, the least good answer) counted towards the score – and so on. Checking the instructions only takes half a minute or so, but is so important.

6. **Work out a rough timetable for the exam, based on the instructions.** This will depend on whether you've got a choice of questions, whether there are compulsory questions, whether all questions carry equal marks or not, and indeed whether you're told to 'Answer Question 1 first, then. . . .' But, for example, suppose the exam started at 09:30, and is going

on till 12:30, and all questions carry equal marks, and you've got to choose any 5 questions from 8. Your rough timetable could be like this:

09:30 'beginning' things – particularly reading the
　　　　questions
09:40 first question (one I like a lot)
10:10 second question (another good one)
10:40 third question (one I know at least some parts of)
11:10 fourth question (one I can get some marks for)
11:40 last question (pick up what I can for this)
12:10 editing and polishing and picking up a lot more
　　　　marks!
12:30 end of exam

All you need to do, of course, is to jot down your target start times for each question. You could well have planned this out in advance in any case, if you knew exactly what the exam structure was going to be, but beware – exam formats sometimes change, and that's why it's important to have read those instructions carefully before committing yourself to a sensible timetable.

7. **Remember that 'equal marks means equal time'.** If, as in the example above, all questions carry equal marks, it's important *not* to spend too long doing your first question, thus not leaving any time to do your last question. If five questions = 100 marks, and you only give yourself time to do four questions, your *maximum* mark is 80. But worse, if you only did three because you spent too long on the first two, say, your *maximum* mark would then only be 60, and in fact your three answers would all have to be *very* good indeed just to pass. And if you only did two – forget it!

8. **Plan in to your timetable some time for checking through your answers.** In the example above, I suggested 20 minutes for this in a 3-hour exam. Even more could be better, but as you'll probably run out of things to say in your last question (where you don't know as much about it, perhaps) there will probably be some further minutes to add to your 'editing and polishing' time.

9. **Ignore the fact that everyone around you appears as if they've already written ten pages!** We're still in the first ten minutes, and you haven't yet *read* the questions properly. But you *have* invested in some sensible planning, and you *have* read the instructions as your basis for this planning. You've already saved more marks than other people have earned – they probably rushed into their first question without any real thought and may come a cropper later!

10. **Now read those questions.** By now, you'll be able to do so much more calmly than a few minutes ago. You've been sensible. You've done your planning. Now it's decision time – if you've got a choice, of course. If you've got no choice – for example if Question 1 is compulsory – it's probably simply best to get on with it straightaway.

11. **Make your choices carefully (if you have choices).** The only way to do this is to read each question properly. You've got to force yourself to read them quite slowly, calmly, deliberately. Work out exactly what the questions mean. Use your highlighter pen to mark the key words such as 'discuss', 'explain', 'list five causes of . . .' and so on, to help you to think through exactly what each question is asking you to do. As you go, make preliminary decisions about each question, for example putting ticks and crosses against them as follows:

✓✓   yes, I reckon I can do this question well.
✓   possibly – I can get at least some marks on this one.
✗   no way – this isn't a question I want to do unless I absolutely have to!

12. **Optional. Make brief notes about things you're frightened you might forget.** Sometimes as you're reading the questions, ideas flood through your mind about things you would wish to make sure you put into your answers. It can sometimes be worth spending a few minutes right then jotting down keywords to remind you of your thoughts. Or jot down a key equation, or a fact or figure or piece of data you might want to include or use, just in case it slips your mind later. If you get into this mode, you might need to go back to your timetable again and knock a few minutes off the time you've

provisionally allowed for each question, to compensate for the time you're now spending organizing your key information for your answers.

13. **Choose to start with a good question.** In other words, start with one where you are confident that you're going to get lots of marks. But beware! Remember your timetable. The big danger is that you'll spend too long on this good question – after all, it's going to be one you know a lot about. Look again very carefully at the question, and decide what you really *need* to include in your answer. You can always add in some more peripheral detail later if you have spare time left.

Answering Questions to Score Marks

This, after all, is the business of doing well at exams. Your aim for the main part of the exam is to get as many marks as you can. This is alongside the aim to lose as few marks as you can. If you already regard this as a game, you're on the right track. If you actually *enjoy* this game, you're probably one of the relatively few people who actually like exams. If, however, this game is not your favourite one, now's the time to find out a little more about some of the rules of the game so that you play the game well when you need to do so. First we'll look at some general points, then in the next sets of tips look more specifically at different types of question: essays and calculations.

1. **Keep, within reasonable limits, to your timetable.** It's important not to write too much about your first couple of questions, where you may indeed have a lot more that you *could* write than would fit into the time you have available.
2. **Build up your stock of marks actually scored.** Most people find it best to do the 'easy' questions first, and to save the 'hard' ones for later. Of course, 'easy' and 'hard' actually depend on how well practised you happen to be for the various questions. When you feel you've got a couple of straightforward questions under your belt – and possibly reached the pass mark for the whole exam – you can then feel a lot more relaxed as you tackle the questions you're not so hot on.
3. **Make good use of any chance to get ahead of schedule.**

For example, if one of your early questions is a problem or calculation, and you're well practised at handling such questions, you may get it completely right (and score all of the available marks) in a lot less than the time you allocated to the question. Then it's worth pressing on, continuing ahead of your schedule, but keeping a watchful eye on the time in case a later question takes more time than you've gained (perhaps because you're struggling with it).

4. **Reread the questions really often as you answer them.** Make sure that you stick to what the questions ask you to do. All of the available marks are linked to exactly what the question asks for. There are no marks at all for things the question *doesn't* ask for. If you don't keep your eye on a question, it's really easy to forget what it asked for, and to waste a lot of time putting down things which, though perfectly correct, won't do you any good.

5. **If there's part of a question you can't answer, get on with the rest of it.** If it happens to be the *first* part of the question that eludes you, leave a space so that you can have a go at it later, and start with the part you're ready to answer – start with marks you *can* score.

6. **When you get stuck, don't try to force yourself on.** For example, if there's something important that you need for a question that just won't come back to you (for example a formula you need for a calculation, or an important name or fact or piece of data), don't try forcing your brain to recall it. That's what causes 'mental blanks' – brains rebel at being cruelly treated and switch off for a while! Almost all mental blanks are caused by owners being cruel to their brains! If you feel yourself getting tenser, now's the time to move on to something you *do* remember. For the moment, forget about your timetable, and move on to another question that you know is going to be straightforward. Most times, the elusive bit of information will filter back into your mind while you're busy doing something else, and will be there when you go back to the original question.

7. **Don't forget to breathe!** Even in an exam, give yourself a minute off now and then, just to let your brain have a rest. Give your thoughts time to settle themselves into sensible

patterns. Give your brain time to think. If you're too busy writing to have time to think, what you write won't be very good.

8. **Make it easy for the examiner.** Examiners are busy people. They may have a huge pile of scripts to mark, and an imminent deadline to meet so that the marks can be processed in time for the exam board. They're working under pressure. They're almost certainly tired. They may well be fed up with seeing students getting things wrong or demonstrating their confusion. They may be depressed. If *your* script is quite easy to mark, because you've laid it out tidily, for example, or because your handwriting is quite good, it makes the examiner's task that bit easier. That makes him or her that bit more favourably disposed towards your answers, and more generous with the marks they give.

9. **Don't give the examiner a headache!** For example, if you write your entire script in bright green ink, this can produce colour fatigue in the examiner's eyes. Someone who's seen a lot of green-on-white may, when looking at the marking scheme (usually black on white), see red blotches in front of their eyes – not good for their generosity index with marks!

10. **Don't write *anything* in red ink.** It's normal for the *examiner* to be using a red pen to mark your script. The examiner may be underlining your mistakes in red – so it's not a good idea for *you* to have underlined your main points in red too! The examiner will be writing in sub-totals and totals in red – so it's not a good idea for you to have written any numbers in red too. It might be thought that if you too are using a red pen for anything, you're invading the examiner's psychological territory – don't take this risk.

11. **Don't go mad with your highlighters.** While it can be useful to use your highlighter on the *question* paper for your own benefit, it can be distracting to use highlighters on your answers. They may even be forbidden by the exam regulations. Besides, scripts are often photocopied for double-marking purposes, or 'moderation', or to send samples to the external examiner. The intended emphasis on anything you've highlighted in your answers may be entirely lost when photocopied.

12. **Ignore the invigilators (unless you need their help).**
Invigilators are there to see that nothing goes wrong with the
exam, and to look after anyone who needs particular help,
and of course to ensure that no unfair practices happen – no
cheating. Don't feel intimidated if you feel they keep looking
at you. They're probably not looking particularly at you at all,
they're just looking around, and you may be nearest.

13. **Put your candidate number and other details on** *any*
further sheets of paper. If you do work on graph sheets, or
extra, loose sheets of paper, or a second exam booklet, make
sure your details are all there too. Don't risk your valuable
work getting separated from your main script or lost – along
with all the marks you've earned.

14. **Don't risk being thought to be cheating.** When you raise
your eyes from your work for a rest, for example, don't look
intently at anyone else. Avoid making eye contact with any
other candidates. Take particular care if you feel any other
candidate is trying to make eye contact with you – look
somewhere else. And don't appear to be reading someone
else's script in front of you or to one side of you – even if your
eyesight is such that you *can* actually read it. Don't move
something you've written to a position on your desk where it
could be more easily read by someone at the side or behind
you. Obviously don't talk to anyone. If you *need* to say
something, raise your hand, keep it raised, and look
expectantly until an invigilator notices and comes up to you.

15. **If you think something is wrong with the exam paper,**
ask an invigilator to investigate. Sometimes, there could be
some data missing from a question. Sometimes, you may not
have been issued with something that is needed to answer a
question. Just occasionally, a question could have been
mistyped somewhere, and simply doesn't make sense. If
anything like this happens, raise your hand, and explain
quietly what you think is wrong to an invigilator. They will
normally make all reasonable efforts to find out whether
indeed something *is* wrong or not. They may have to go out
and telephone the original question-setter. They may have to
send for someone else to come and decide if there is a
problem or not. If something *is* wrong, an announcement may

eventually be made to all of the candidates for that particular exam. But while this is all going on, don't sit and wait and wait and wait – get on with another question where there is no problem. Continue to chase marks while the problem is being investigated.

Essays in Exams

In some subjects, all or most of your answers will be in essay format. We've already looked at various aspects of how best to put together essays for coursework requirements. Though many of the same factors continue to apply to writing essays in exams, there are significant differences – for a start, you haven't got much opportunity for drafting and redrafting in an exam. The following tips should help you to score as many marks as you can for essay-type exam questions.

1. **Read the questions even more carefully.** One problem with essays in exams is that there can sometimes be several ways of interpreting the question or title you're given. It's important to decide really thoroughly what the question is

most likely to mean. What sorts of answers will whoever set the question be expecting? Where will the marks be available? How much do you know about what is being looked for? It's much better to spend an extra few minutes deciding whether a particular question is really a good one for you, than to rush in blindly and only halfway through realize you would have been better off doing a different question.

2. **Make sensible adjustments to your timetable for the exam.** For example, you might only have three essays to write in three hours, but by the time you've read the questions well enough to make your various choices, half an hour might have gone. You still need to save time for editing and polishing at the end, so allow up to half an hour for that, and divide the remaining time by three, to work out how much time to spend on each essay.

3. **Plan your essay answers.** Even in an exam, it's worth spending a few minutes mapping out how you're going to structure an essay. The 'lay an egg' idea discussed in the tips on essays in this book works well, done in miniature, in an exam. Five minutes gathering your thoughts for an essay, and working out in which order you're going to present these thoughts, is time well spent. It will *save* you more than five minutes when you get on writing the essay. It will also earn you more marks than you would have scored if you'd just ploughed on into the essay without thinking.

4. **Don't necessarily keep your essay plan to yourself.** Sometimes it's worth putting your plan right there in your answer booklet, before the start of your essay. Find out what lecturers think of this idea and, if they approve, adopt this practice in exams. Clearly, if they *don't* approve, make your jottings on spare paper or at the back of your exam booklet. Including a plan of an essay does show that you didn't just rush into it. Sometimes (for example if time runs out on you) an examiner might look back at your plan to see what else you might have included in your essay had you had time. This could even lead to the odd extra mark.

5. **The introduction to your answer is crucial.** This is what will set the examiner's expectations. There's no second chance to make that good first impression. Therefore, it's

worth doing your introduction really carefully. Your introduction needs to be lived up to by the rest of your essay. Don't introduce important things that you won't have time to return to and discuss properly.

6. **Consider *not* writing your introduction till last!** As with coursework essays, the ideal time to write the beginning of an essay is when you already know what you actually did in the main body of the essay, and where that led you. You can still do this in an exam, especially if you've practised doing this. For example, you can leave some space for what is going to be your first paragraph, and then add it in when you've more or less finished the rest of the essay. This does need some editorial skills – you need to be able to squeeze or stretch your introduction to fit into the space you've left for it.

7. **Don't go chasing the last few marks for an essay-type answer.** Suppose the question carries 20 marks. It's relatively easy to get the first 8 marks or so – even if you don't know a great deal about the topic – as long as what you write addresses the question as asked. But it's very rare for even a wonderful answer to be awarded 20 out of 20 for an essay. A really good one tends to get 16 or 17. So it's just not worth spending an extra half-hour going after those elusive last few marks.

8. **Keep your sentences relatively short and simple.** Even the most complex ideas can be expressed in short sentences. The problem with *long* sentences in exam answers is that there's more chance of your meaning not getting across to the examiner. There's also more chance in a long sentence that you end up saying something *different* from what you actually mean. Another problem with really long sentences is that the examiner may have to read them several times to work out what you were trying to say. This slows the examiner up – and doesn't do much for his or her 'generosity index'!

Calculations and Problems

There are several differences between calculation-type questions and essays. Sometimes you'll have a choice where you can select some essays and some calculations. The more you know about how to tackle both sorts of questions the better. If, of course, you *only* do essay-type exams, don't bother with the tips that follow now.

1.   **Remember that for calculation-type questions, you may be able to get *all* of the marks.** If you get the right answer in such questions, you can score 20 out of 20. In such questions there's no way that marks could be deducted if you got it perfectly right. So if you've got a choice between an essay and a calculation, and you *know* you'll have no difficulty with the calculation, it can be worth choosing the calculation question. On the other hand, if you are not sure you can get the calculation question right, you could be safer with the essay.

2.   **Check whether you can *really* do the question.** One of the difficulties with numerical questions is that it's possible to struggle for a long time and get nowhere. If you can't 'crack' the question, you may end up with no marks. Sometimes it takes a little while to work out whether or not you're going to be able to crack the question. If you have already practised regularly on just such a question, you will have a much better idea whether the question is going to be a safe bet for you.

3.   **Be particularly careful with timing.** Suppose you have five

numerical questions to tackle in a three-hour exam. That boils down, as I've already said in previous tips, to half an hour per question, plus the 'getting started' activities plus the 'editing' time to be left for the end of the exam. But with numerical questions, timing is more variable. If you're really practised at handling a particular sort of question, you may be able to completely finish it in as little as 10 minutes or less. You may have scored *all* of the marks in that short time. But with another question where you get bogged down in the calculations, you might not have got to your answer by the end of 30 minutes. You might not even have scored *any* marks for that question yet.

4. **Plan your strategy.** For example, after you've decided which questions you're going to attempt, it can be worth doing all the *easy* bits of these questions first – picking up all of the marks that are straightforward to score. Then you could go on to tackle in turn the harder bits of each question, rationing your time so that you allow equal time for equal possible marks as normal.

5. **Let the examiner see exactly how you tackled numerical calculations.** As mentioned above, if you get a numerical question completely right, you could get all of the available marks. But if you get the *wrong* answer, you could end up with *none* of the marks. That's a lot of difference! This is much more than the difference between a brilliant essay and a mediocre one. What about if you do it partly right, but don't end up with the right answer? If so, you could get *most* of the marks – or *none* of the marks, depending entirely on one thing: *whether the examiner can work out exactly what you did.* If the examiner can *see* exactly where you went wrong, and can *see* that everything else you did was right, you'll get most of the marks, even with the wrong final answer. If the examiner *can't see* where you went wrong, you'll get no marks. So show *how* you did the calculation. Show the equation you used for your calculation. Then *show* which numbers you substituted into the equation for each piece of data you used.

6. **Make graphs and diagrams big enough.** You're not being charged extra for using more paper. Sometimes a self-explanatory diagram or sketch graph can tell the examiner

that you *know* what you're writing about better than words could have done. More importantly, it's often *faster* to illustrate something by putting in a sketch than it would be to explain it all in words.

7. **Label your diagrams or graphs.** With graphs, you'll always lose marks if axes aren't labelled, if scales aren't sensibly chosen and marked up, and so on. With diagrams, label the various parts clearly, so the diagram becomes self-explanatory. Consider saying 'see figure 3' in your answer to refer the examiner to a diagram, just as you would if you were writing an article, not forgetting to give the diagram a caption 'Figure 3: sketch of. . . .'.

8. **With calculations, pay attention to the number of significant figures you use in your answers.** For example, you may go through a complex calculation, and your calculator gives you the number 3120.86. By the time you combine together the experimental errors in the data you've used along the way, the sensible way to express the answer might be 3100 plus-or-minus 200, meaning somewhere between 2900 and 3300. This could be written 3100 ± 200. In numerical questions, you can *always* assume that you will actually *lose* marks every time you write down a final answer that still includes too many significant figures. It is, of course, acceptable to write down the actual numbers as read from your calculator in your 'working out'.

9. **If you get really stuck with a numerical question, move on to something else.** It's dangerous to keep on struggling, thinking 'I'm sure I can do this – I'll just give it another try' for too long. The minutes will be ticking away. You won't get any further marks until you either solve the problem, or score some marks for something else altogether.

Towards the End of
Each Exam

I've stressed all along the importance of leaving some time to do various things towards the end of each exam. For example, leave 20 minutes or so for a 3-hour exam, perhaps even more. You may, in fact, gain *more marks* in these 20 minutes than you did in any other 20 minutes during the whole exam. In other words, your 'marks-scored-per-minute' tally may be highest during these final minutes. These extra marks can, of course, make all the difference between a fail and a pass grade, or between a quite-good score and a really-good score. It's up to you – no one can *make* you do what is sensible at the end of each exam. But in the tips that follow, I hope to convince you to adopt some sensible tactics to make the most of your closing minutes in each exam.

1. **If you've finished, resist the temptation to leave.** You may be allowed to leave – and the world outside seems a much more appealing place. You may be really wanting to escape now. You may be hungry or thirsty or both. You may want to have a sleep! There may be people all around you handing in their scripts and escaping. But if you go before doing the things suggested below, you've lost the chance of gaining any more marks. As soon as you're outside, you may suddenly remember the fact that was eluding you that you'd wanted to include in Question 3. You may then think of something you'd misquoted in Question 2. You may recall that you still hadn't written down your interpretation of the answer you got for

Question 5. All too late now – there's nothing you can do about it once you've left.

2. **You may not be *allowed* to leave, anyway.** Some institutions have a policy that no-one can leave during the last half-hour of an exam, as too many people moving around could disturb other people who are still working away at answering the questions.

3. **If you've not yet finished, stop!** Tempting as it is just to keep on answering the questions, there are things to do now which will score you *more* marks. If, for example, you're still in the final stage of an essay-type answer, you will probably just be chasing those elusive marks towards the top of the range for that question. You might already have scored 14 out of 20, and may only get one more mark if you carried on with that essay till time was up. Or you might have scored 8 out of 20 and may still only upgrade this to 9 out of 20 by all your further efforts over the next 20 minutes. After all, this is your *last* question, and will probably be your least good answer anyway.

4. **Don't *just* stop, however.** Round off what you were writing about so that it looks as though you didn't just stop! Come to a conclusion. Restate your main finding. Underline the answer you've just calculated. And so on. But for no more than a couple of minutes. Then *do* stop!

5. **Take a deep breath or two, and relax for a short while.** Stretch your legs (and arms, if it's not too noticeable). Give your brain time to settle. You're going to need it again very shortly.

6. **Accept that you don't really *want* to do what you're going to do next, but that it will be worth it!** You're going to go back and look at everything you've been doing since you started your first answer. You know it makes sense.

7. **Do it.** Go straight back to your first answer and read it right through, with your pen firmly in your hand. Look back at the question as you start, then, as you read . . .

8. **. . . make additions.** Things will have surfaced in your mind that weren't in your mind hours ago when you wrote your original answer. Some of these things will be worth marks. Put them in now. Squeeze them in between your paragraphs.

Where necessary, put 'please see page 9' with *, then **, then ***, then ϕ, then θ – it doesn't matter how many symbols you end up using, so long as the examiner can *find* where you've slipped in important extra little bits. Carry on doing this, and also . . .

9. **. . . make corrections.** You'll often notice sentences that don't read as you meant them to read. Sometimes you might have written the exact opposite of what you meant! You get marks for what you actually wrote – not what you meant. The examiner isn't psychic. So now's the time to make sure that what's on your script is what you meant. And also . . .

10. **. . . make adjustments.** In particular, do anything you can to make it easier for the examiner to mark your answers. For example, make it really clear where each question starts and ends, and where you start each new part in the questions which have separate parts. Make headings and main points stand out that little bit more clearly. And also . . .

11. **. . . firm-up conclusions.** It can sometimes be well worth making it really clear where each question ends by (for example) firmly stating the result of a calculation, rather than just having the final number at the bottom of it. Make sure that in essay-type answers your final paragraph is really bringing your answer to a solid ending. Remember that the *end* of your answer to any question is the last thing the examiner sees before working out how many marks to give that answer. Make a favourable last impression – good endings lead to better marks. And perhaps . . .

12. **. . . dredge up missing information from your memory.** Now that the exam's almost over, and you've scored all the extra marks by doing the wise actions above, you can risk a little cruelty to your brain, if there are still some things eluding you. You're hardly likely to force yourself into a mental blank with only minutes to go – and even if you did, it wouldn't really matter any more.

13. **If somewhere in the exam you made a false start, make your intentions really clear.** Suppose you made a false start at Question 3, and subsequently went on to do a really good answer to Question 8 instead, it's important that your false start is crossed out, otherwise Assessment Regulations

normally mean that you'd be assessed on the *first* five questions you answered (including your false start), not the *best* five. Don't, however, *obliterate* your false start. It's still just possible that if a 'benefit of the doubt' decision is needed (for example if you're on a borderline), your crossed-out attempt might be taken into account, and may sway the balance in your favour.

14. **Check again that your details are on any loose pages.** You don't want the credit you got for a graph, or the extra thinking you put onto some additional loose paper, to get lost.

15. **When you've done all of the things above, go back to completing any unfinished answers.** Now that you've scored all of those extra marks for additions and corrections to the questions you've already done, you can afford the time to chase those elusive marks on questions you've not yet finished.

16. **If there's still time left, and you've completed everything above, sit and relax.** Try to avoid the growing temptation to leave (if you're allowed to leave). Keep looking back through your work now and then, seeing if there are any further corrections, additions and adjustments you can still make. You may still get the odd flash of inspiration and think of something that's worth some marks, in time to put it in. Such inspiration is no use at all to you once you've handed in your script.

After an Exam

This is the moment you've been looking forward to ever since the start of the exam – and for weeks or months longer than that. Now it's arrived. Now you're out of the exam room. You're free. The exam is over. You can be human again. So why am I giving you some tips for things to do *after* an exam? Read on to find out.

1. **Nothing that you can do now can make any difference whatsoever to the mark you've just scored.** The exam is now history. Your mark is now fixed, be it a good one or a bad one. That said, there are some things it's worth making sure that you *don't* do now.

2. **Avoid the post-mortem.** Yes, that particular exam *is* dead, but there's not a single mark to be gained by finding out now how you could have given better answers to those exam questions. A post-mortem would use up a lot of mental energy you can't afford to spare, especially if you've got more exams coming soon. After your *last* exam you can have an extended post-mortem, if that's really the sort of thing which turns you on. But don't do it if you've got more exams coming up. Why not? . . .

3. **A post-mortem will depress you!** True, you'll find comfort when you work out that your answer to Question 3 was a good one. But the trouble with post-mortems is that you'll also get nasty surprises. You'll find out all sorts of things that you *didn't* get round to including in your answers. In fact, it's the nasty surprises that will get to you.

4. **Avoid talking to other people who did the same exam.** There's no problem talking to people who've just done *another* exam. But if you talk to people who've just done *your* exam, you'll find out successful things they did, which you *didn't* do – which will score marks for them. You may also find out about mistakes *they* made which you didn't make – but you'll probably not think much about these as you're too busy worrying about the mistakes *you* made which they didn't make.

5. **Don't let other people depress you.** There are some people who seem to take delight in taking the wind out of your sails. Perhaps it makes them feel better? But if you *did* make some ghastly mistakes in the exam you've just done, and you don't actually know about them, isn't it best to *continue* not knowing about them, at least for the present? The only time it's worth finding out more about those mistakes is when the same kinds of mistakes may be relevant to the *next* exams.

6. **Some people get so upset by a post-mortem that they fail their *next* exam.** If you get discouraged by all the things that you find out from a post-mortem, it could damage your

confidence for your next exam, and lose you marks in that one too. It could also damage the revision you do between now and that next exam.

7. **Don't waste the energy.** It actually consumes a lot of energy to do a post-mortem. Think of it! Do you *enjoy* exams so much that it gives you a lot of pleasure to relive the whole event, and this time in slow motion? There are far happier things to do with your energy.

8. **'But I'm not ready to relax yet.'** True. You've got extra adrenalin still in your system, and it's not easy to switch off and relax. But don't dissipate all of that extra adrenalin in something as useless as a post-mortem – invest in your *next* exam right now, instead.

9. **Do a little gentle revision for your next exam.** Dig out your question bank for the subject that's coming up next, and quietly remind yourself of what you already know, and identify a few things which will shortly need a little polishing up. This isn't hard work, but it's tuning your mind in to what's coming next, rather than dwelling on what's history now.

10. **Do some tidying up and sorting out.** Put away the things you no longer need, and dig out the things you'll need for your preparations for the next exam. Make space for the next stage of your work.

11. **Let the new knowledge flush out the memories of the old knowledge.** Doing a little gentle revision helps you get the feeling that you've already moved forward from that previous exam, and you're heading purposefully towards the next one. Soon you'll have a rest, but for now you're doing something really sensible and logical.

12. **Pause to think about what you've learned about *processes* from your last exam.** This is probably the *only* time when it's useful to think back to the exam that's passed. Was your time management OK in that exam? If not, think how you'll take steps to improve it in your next one. Did you get a lot out of those final minutes when you made additions and corrections? Remind yourself to do this next time too. Regard each exam as a chance to learn more about how best *you* can develop your skills at the game of being a successful candidate. Learn from what worked well for you, and also

from things that didn't work out as you wanted them to. But keep it general – *don't* now go and try to work out what the answer to Question 3 really was!

13. **Make plans for your next stage of revision.** Look at how best to spend the time between now and your next exam. Don't forget to continue to plan in breaks, and variety, and so on. Remind yourself which topics are going to need a bit more time than others.

14. **Now enjoy being smug!** Other people who took that last exam will still be indulging in their post-mortems, and here are you, nicely recovered from that exam, and already on your way towards your next one. Now you deserve that well-earned break. Build up your own reward system. However, don't plan a grade 1 hangover as an integral part of your reward system – at least not until we're talking about what to do after your *last* exam!

Open-book Exams

Many of the tips in the sections covered already continue to apply to other sorts of exam. There are in fact several different kinds of exam, and there are some differences in how best to revise for them, and how best to do them when you meet them. The following suggestions will help you fine-tune your revision and exam techniques for the particular circumstances of open-book exams.

1. **Don't say to yourself: 'It will be easy, I'll have the books in there with me.'** Yes, you will, but the big danger is that you could end up spending too much of your time in the exam *reading* the book rather than answering the questions. You only get marks for what you *write*. Of course you do need to do some reading in an open-book exam, but very quickly, and in a highly structured and practised way. You need to do *most* of your reading *before* the exam itself.

2. **Get really familiar with the books you'll be able to use in your exam.** Open-book exams normally allow candidates to have a predefined range of textbooks and/or printed materials on the exam desk. Normally, you'll know in advance exactly what these will be. When this is so, make sure that you know your way around these books really well long before the exam.

3. **Find out whether the books are going to be issued in the exam room.** Sometimes a whole set of the same books is used, so that all candidates have exactly the same books.

Alternatively it could be up to you to bring in your own books, and you might have some choice about which books you bring in. But in any case, remember that there will be limits regarding how much you can carry in with you, and a limited amount of space on your exam desk.

4. **Find out whether you'd be allowed to bring in notes as well.** In open-book exams, you are sometimes allowed to use *any* reference material you want, including your own summaries and notes.

5. **If it's up to you to take in books, get your hands on them early!** The library copies may soon all be booked out. The bookshop may soon sell out of those books. In any case, you need to have copies of the books for long enough to get really comfortable using them.

6. **Sort out which *parts* of the books are going to be relevant.** Cross-match the books with your syllabus, the intended learning outcomes, and where possible with old open-book exam questions. Normally, you'll find that some parts of the books may be quite tangential to the exam questions, but other parts will be directly relevant – get to know these parts.

7. **Get fast at *finding things* using the book.** If you know a book well, it takes you far less time to use the contents pages and index to track down exactly which pages are relevant to a particular topic or question. The faster you are at finding the relevant pages there and then in the exam room, the more time you'll have to answer the questions. You don't get any marks until you put pen to paper!

8. **In your revision, practise *using* the book to answer questions.** This is quite different from answering questions out of your head. You'll still need to use your memory, and to link things in the books to things you already know from elsewhere. But in an open-book exam, you're expected to be able to answer the exam questions in the particular context of material that's on your desk in that particular book.

9. **Allow yourself reading time.** In this sort of exam, it's not just reading the questions you need to allow time for. You also need to allow for a reasonable amount of time to look things up in the books.

10. **In the exam, don't just copy things down out of the books.** If, for example, everyone is using the *same* book in the exam, all you may need to do is to reference the page number and paragraph, then write down what *you* make of an idea or concept from the book, rather than copy it all out and then comment upon it. You won't get any marks for things you directly copy out, so it would be a waste of your time and energy to do so.

11. **Put clear references down, showing where you found particular things in the books.** The author and title of the books may be common to all of your references, and may just need writing out in full when you make your first references in each question. But it is possible that there are different editions of a particular book, and that the same bit of the book appears on differently numbered pages of the respective editions, so make sure that it will be possible for the examiner to see exactly what you were referring to each time you use something from a book.

12. **As always, read the questions really well.** The questions in an open-book exam are normally quite different from those in traditional exams. You're expected to be able to *discuss* things that are already in the books, and *comment* on them and *make decisions* about them, and *apply* them, and so on, not just to describe what's in the book.

'Seen' Written Exams

This is yet another variety of exam, where you are given the questions in advance. Usually, if you have this sort of exam at all, you'll be given the questions only a relatively short time before the exam itself. You may be given the questions exactly as they will appear on the exam paper, or you may be given some information *about* the questions. There's usually the same kind of time constraint as in normal exams, but there are no surprises regarding the questions themselves. Many of the tips already given in this book about revision and exams continue to apply, but there are a few differences too.

1. **Get practising straight away.** If you know in advance what the exam questions are, your revision can be directly related to answering those particular questions. It's worth getting started with this as soon as you're given the questions. As with any other time-constrained activity, the more often you've *practised* answering a particular question, the better you'll do it for real when you need to.

2. **Find out which questions you're going to be best at answering.** This applies particularly if there's a choice. The best way to find out is by experience. Sometimes a question *looks* easy to answer, but when you get pen and paper to work, it turns out to be harder. So try your hand at *all* of the questions, before deciding which you're really going to concentrate on in your revision.

3. **Work out what's *really relevant* to each question.** One of

the problems with 'seen' exams is that it's easy to find out so much about each question that you could sit and write for hours. But you'll have at least two or three questions to answer, probably more. The danger of spending too long on one question has never been greater than in this kind of exam.

4. **Make egg diagrams.** As with writing coursework essays, it can be really useful for you to map out exactly how you're going to answer a known question, and to build up (and whittle down) your map on the basis of your growing experience of expressing your answer to that question as you continue to prepare for it.

5. **It's no use just *knowing* how to answer the questions.** In a 'seen' exam, as in any other exam, the marks you get are for what you write. You can know something backwards, but still take ages to put down what you know in writing.

6. **Practise *writing out* answers to the questions.** Use *timed* practice, until you find out realistically what you can do in half-an-hour or an hour, depending how long you'll have for each question.

7. **Use practise to gain speed.** The more often you've practised answering a question, the less time you have to sit and think about each sentence you write in your answer. In turn, this means that you can write more in your answers (which is especially important if you are slow at handwriting).

8. **Be really fussy about sticking exactly to the questions.** When you've done some practice answers to the question, look back at the question and decide what the marking scheme might look like. Go through your answers looking for anything that doesn't exactly match what was asked for by the question – and delete it!

9. **Keep practising, and increase the *quality* of your answers, not the length.** In the exam itself, you won't have time to write really long answers in any case. It will be really important for you to match the time you spend with each question to the marks available for it.

10. **Make informed decisions about which questions you'll tackle in the exam (if you *have* a choice, of course).** Only when you've done some practising can you make such

decisions well. Sometimes what *seemed* like a straightforward question proves difficult to answer. Sometimes what looked like a hard question turns out to be straightforward.

11. **Consider working with fellow-students for some of your revision.** For example, if you look at their practice answers and they at yours, you can all gain a lot from the different ways you tackled the questions. This means that in the real exam, you can all do better – you're unlikely to be using exactly the same words and sentences then and risk being accused of cheating.

12. **In the exam itself, read the questions carefully.** They *may* be exactly as you were led to believe them to be. But what if they are slightly different? What if some extra points have been added? What if some extra choices have been added? Don't just assume that you already know what the questions are – it only takes a minute or two to double-check.

13. **Give yourself time to breathe in the exam.** Your head may well be full of everything you intend to put down on paper for the questions you've prepared to answer. But no one can write solidly and *well* for hours on end. Make sure that you still allow time to *think* about how best to convey your meaning.

14. **Still allow some time for editing and polishing at the end of the exam.** Seen written exams are no different from traditional unseen ones in this respect. You can still gain valuable marks by going back to what you've written, and making sure that what you *meant* is what you wrote.

Multiple-choice Exams

In some ways these are quite different from written exams – for a start, you may not have to write anything! Multiple-choice exams take various forms, and there's more about these in the tips below. They're often used as part of a mixture of different kinds of assessment in a course. You may already be familiar with this kind of testing, but if not, the following tips should help you prepare for such exams systematically, and tackle them logically when you meet them. I'll start with some questions you may be asking yourself about such exams.

1. **'What *are* multiple-choice exams?'** Normally, they're fairly short, structured questions, each of which contains options from which you are to select the best one – or the correct one. There may be four options for each question – sometimes more. The best (or correct) option scores you the mark for that question. The other options may score you no marks at all – perhaps even 'negative' marks!
2. **'What are these *other* options?'** They are called 'distractors'. They are traps! They may *look* as though they're right. They may indeed be *partly* right, but not as good as the correct option. Distractors are meant to be *plausible*. They're meant to be selected by candidates who don't know enough to tell the difference between the right (or best) option and the distractors.
3. **'What do I actually *do* in a multiple-choice exam?'** This depends. Some multiple-choice exams are done sitting at a

computer keyboard. A question, along with the options, from which you select one, appears on the screen. You use the mouse to click the option you think is the right one, and then the next question appears, and so on.

4. **'What, an exam with no pen?'** Yes, if it's a computer-based exam. But you can also have multiple-choice exams done on paper. This time you'll need a pen or pencil, to put a tick or cross into the box beside the option you pick for each question. Or, more often, you'll have the questions with their options on printed sheets and a special card with boxes for you to mark. This card is then fed into an optical mark reader, which works out your score for the exam.

5. **The best way to revise for multiple-choice exams is to do lots of them.** In other words, get your hands on multiple-choice questions to practise on. These may already exist, for example on computer software that you can access on an intranet. They may exist on paper too. But the best way to get skilled at multiple-choice tests is to make up questions of your own, and practise with these. And – even better – do it with your friends, and quiz each other with your questions.

6. **Multiple-choice exams measure speed.** This time, of course, it's not speed of writing down answers. These exams measure how fast you *think*. In particular, they measure how fast you *make decisions* about which options are best and which ones are wrong. Such speed is, of course, gained in the usual way – through practice.

7. **Multiple-choice exams measure how well you read the questions!** Usually, there will be lots of questions – 50 or 100, for example. Each with four (or five) options to select from – that's a lot of reading. So it's worth becoming faster at reading the questions and options *well*.

8. **Multiple-choice exams are tiring.** This is because you're making one decision after another – all the time. 'Is this option the right one?' 'Is this option just a distractor?' 'If so, what's wrong with it?' and so on. In just an hour in a multiple-choice exam, your mind can be ranging through far more subject material than you could possibly have *written* about in a three-hour exam. That's a lot of thinking!

9. **Before a multiple-choice exam, find out all you can**

about exactly what you have to do. If it's a computer-based exam, you'll normally have some chance to practise until you know exactly what to do with the machine. If it's a paper-based exam in a normal exam room, with optically readable cards to fill in, it's useful for you to get your hands on such a card and work out exactly how to fill it in. For example, you may need to enter your candidate number and other details in little boxes as optically readable pencil marks, as well as your choices of options. Since your handwriting won't normally be on the card, if you don't enter your details correctly, no one will be able to tell after the exam that it was *your* card – and you wouldn't get any marks!

10. **During the exam, keep your cool.** Don't try to rush too fast, or you may find yourself getting flustered by all the thinking you're doing. Tackle one question at a time, as follows.

11. **Read the question, and each option, carefully.** Watch out – there may only be a single word *wrong* in a particular option that turns it into a distractor. For example, the little word 'not' can make all the difference!

12. **If you *know* that a particular option is the right one, choose it.** Then just check quickly that the other options are not right – or not *as* right. That's that question sorted out.

13. **If you *think* that a particular option may be the right one, think about the distractors before making your decision.** If you can *see* what's wrong with all of the *other* options, the one you think is the right one is probably the right one after all. So choose it.

14. **If you're not at all sure about a question, try a process of elimination.** Look at all of the options, and try to find one that is definitely *not* correct. This is likely to be a distractor. Now look for *another* that is suspect. If at the end of this there's only one option that *doesn't* seem to have anything wrong with it, it's a fair bet that this will be the right one to choose.

15. **Make the most of any freedom you have.** For example, in paper-based multiple-choice exams (with or without optically readable cards), you may be able to go backwards and forwards through the questions in any order you choose. If

you have this freedom, you might prefer to do all the *easy* questions first (the questions where you *know* which is the best option), so that you feel you've already got a lot of the available marks under your belt. Then you can slow down and spend your energy on the harder questions, where you're going to have to think harder about which options are the distractors. With computer-based multiple-choice exams, you may not have such freedom, and may have to answer the questions in the order in which they appear on your screen.

16. **At the end of the exam, check that you've done everything you need to have done.** For example, in paper-based exams, is your candidate number (and any other details) entered correctly? In a computer-based exam, have you logged off, if instructed?

Preparing for Your Re-sit

Preparing for a re-sit wasn't part of your plans! However, you could find yourself in this position – many people do – perhaps through no fault of your own, due to unavoidable circumstances and so on. The most sensible thing to do is to prepare for it in a constructive and logical way. The following suggestions are about preparing for a re-sit in a traditional exam; you can easily extend them to any other exam format.

1. **Accept the situation.** There's nothing to be gained by feeling resentful or sorry for yourself – this will just waste mental energy. This isn't the time to go round saying to yourself 'If only I'd revised more' or 'If only I'd done Question 3 instead of Question 5' and so on.
2. **Don't regard it as a major setback.** When you're successful with your re-sit, you're then back on course, along with the people who didn't have any re-sits. You're a little wiser than you would have been, however. You know more about preparing for exams, and how to pass this particular kind of exam.
3. **Remind yourself it could have been worse.** You might have had to repeat a whole year – one or two re-sits are a lot less wasteful of your time and energy. The fact that you've been *allowed* to re-sit an exam means that you're thought to be able to succeed in it.
4. **Use it as a learning opportunity.** Now's your chance to learn some of the things you hadn't mastered before. Perhaps

this time you've only got one or two exams to prepare for, rather than a whole set. There may be some aspects of the subject which were just too difficult for you to tackle in the time available previously, and now's another chance to have a go at these using a more structured approach.

5. **Look back at what might have gone wrong with the exam first time round.** Although in general there's no mileage in post-mortems, it's different if an exam wasn't successful. Look to see whether it was your speed that wasn't up to it. Did you run out of time? Or was it just that you didn't know enough at the time? Or was it that you weren't practised enough at doing particular kinds of answer? Or perhaps you'd learnt 'the wrong things' and what you'd learnt wasn't asked for on the exam paper?

6. **Make the most of any opportunity to get feedback on your past exam.** Some universities allow students to see their marked scripts. This can be useful to discover exactly which questions caused you to lose marks. Alternatively, your lecturers may be willing to give you some informal feedback, and give you some suggestions about things it could be useful for you to focus on next time. But don't make a nuisance of yourself in your quest to find out about what might have gone wrong.

7. **Go back through that old exam paper.** Work out exactly what you *didn't* know, with reference to the questions. In fact, it can be useful at this stage to spend some time writing full answers to the questions on that paper, just to help you to find out exactly what led to you having to re-sit that exam.

8. **Was there a question you got thoroughly stuck on?** That's one of the most common causes of people failing an exam. Perhaps you spent far longer than you should have done on that question, and still got nowhere with it, and then didn't have enough time to spare for the other questions. If there was such a question, now's your chance to really crack it. Find out how to do it – ask other people if you can't solve it yourself. Then *practise* doing it, until you can tackle that particular question in minutes. The same sort of question may well be on your re-sit paper too.

9. **Remember that the re-sit paper is expected to be of the**

same standard. You might even get one or two questions that are very similar to the ones in the original paper.

10. **Look carefully at the original paper, and work out what** *didn't* **come up that time.** Which bits of the syllabus were missed by that particular exam? Possibly these were the bits you already knew well, of course! The probability is that the re-sit paper will include at least some such questions.

11. **Aim to be primed for a comfortable pass.** While you might think, 'I want to show them!', it's normal that a re-sit is simply marked as pass or fail. So don't worry too much about doing brilliantly in the re-sit; rather, make sure that whatever happens you're going to be nicely above the pass mark.

12. **Aim to be able to** *know* **you've passed, halfway through the exam.** For example, don't spend ages on your first question because you happen to be really clued up on it – just plan to get on answering the question as asked, rather than spending a lot of time on it. You can always come back and put down more later, but your main job is to make sure you've passed the whole exam first, so move on systematically until you've answered *all* of the questions.

13. **Focus your revision on practising answering questions.** That's what's going to be measured in your re-sit – as in any other exam. The more practised you are, the faster you are, and the less time you need to sit and think, and the more time you can put pen to paper and score marks.

14. **Build plenty of repetition into your revision.** Every time you practise answering a particular sort of question, you get faster at it as well as better at it. Some things just can't be learnt properly without doing them over and over again. But repeat things on different days, rather than ten times on one day.

15. **When possible, spend some revision time with other people preparing for the same re-sit exam.** If you can pool your experiences of what went wrong, what you didn't know well enough at the time of the original exam, and so on, you'll all be better at making sure that you pass the re-sit. It's also quite reassuring to spend time with other people who are tackling exactly the same situation as you are.

16. **Don't put off starting your re-sit revision.** Get straight

into it as soon as you know you've got a re-sit. One of the problems is that not everyone you know will be revising this time round, so you'll need to build yourself ways of taking time out from other things you do, and fit in sufficient revision time.

17. **When you come to the exam, read the questions really carefully.** All of the tips on exams continue to apply, of course, so have another look through these and work out which ones you intend to focus on for your re-sit. But, in particular, make sure that if you've got a choice of questions in your re-sit, you choose really well, and select the questions which will see you safely beyond the pass mark. Also, ensure that you have *really* worked out exactly what each of your selected questions is asking you to do – and do that, and *only* that, in your answers.

Part VIII

Job Hunting

Writing Your Curriculum Vitae

This is your best starting point towards job hunting. It's never too early to start this. Make it one of your priorities to get to the position where you have an up-to-date CV (curriculum vitae) on a computer, on a back-up disk or two, and with one or two printed copies flat in a large envelope (to keep them clean) in a drawer. Do this now, or soon, as long as you don't do it as a work-avoidance strategy for something even more important, such as revision. What's a CV? What should it do for you? How can you keep it well maintained? Read on.

1. **What's your CV?** Essentially, it's the story of your life. More particularly, it's about your education, your experience, and all of your good points. It's something to send to prospective employers when you apply for jobs. It's something to send in along with application forms, even if you're not asked for a CV. If you have a job, it's something to use when you want a better one, or a promotion.

2. **How big should my CV be?** Your CV will grow with your career. At first, it could be as compact as a single A4 sheet, when in print. Even when you've a lot of relevant employment history and experience, it shouldn't be more than about 4 sides of A4 – if it's *too* long, people won't read it!

3. **What's special about a CV?** The real advantage is that your CV is under *your* control. You are in charge of what's in it, how it looks, how long it is, in which order you present yourself, and everything else. You're playing the job-hunting

game on 'home ground'. With application forms, it's 'away
territory' – the employer is in charge of most of these things.

4. **Have a look at other people's CVs.** There are many
   different approaches to choose from. You can, with a word
   processor, make radical changes to the order and structure of
   your CV in just a few minutes, for example if you happen to
   see someone else's, and wish to adopt some of its features.

5. **Work out what you want your CV to do for you.** Work
   out what impression you want to make with it. This will help
   you decide on its size, order, content and style. The main
   purpose of your CV is to be a passport towards getting shortlisted for interview when you apply for jobs.

6. **An up-to-date, accurate CV can save you hours!** When
   you're job-hunting seriously, you could be filling in countless
   application forms. On each of these, you'll need accurate
   details of exam dates, qualifications, employment history (if
   any) as well as contact details and so on. If they're all
   contained in this one document, and they're all kept up to
   date as a matter of routine, all you need to do is pull out your
   CV and use it to speed up the process of filling in those
   application forms.

7. **Start with the factual information.** This includes your full
   name, date of birth, place of birth, nationality, address,
   marital status, contact telephone numbers, email address if
   you have one, and so on. Give date of birth rather than age –
   the date doesn't change, your age does!

8. **Continue with details of your education and
   qualifications.** Include as much detail as may be wanted by
   employers: exams passed along with the year(s) in which you
   passed them and the grades or marks, and which examining
   bodies were involved. Also include the qualifications you're
   presently heading for with *estimated* date of being awarded
   them. Make it clear that these are *anticipated* qualifications at
   present, of course – don't claim them as if you already had
   them.

9. **Next, write a section on 'Employment and Experience'.**
   For example, if you've had vacation jobs or part-time jobs
   while you've been a student, put down some details. Make it
   clear that you've already been found to be employable, and

have held down paid work. Emphasise that you're the sort of person who could regularly get out of bed in the morning and not be sacked for absenteeism or unpunctuality! Put contact details of any employers who may be happy to vouch for you or confirm what you say. Make a point of mentioning any positions of trust or responsibility you may have held in connection with your past employment. If, of course, you've not yet had *any* such experience, simply don't include such a section at all – it's *your* CV.

10. **Career aims.** It's useful to include a short section, telling about what your present overall plans are for your future career. Obviously, don't say that you're looking for a lot of money for a little work! Include some details of *what* interests you, and *why* you're interested in particular things, and why you think you will be *good* at particular kinds of work.

11. **What about hobbies, leisure interests, recreation?** Compose a section along these lines to make it clear that you're a normal, sociable human being. Allow it to be seen that you're fit and healthy (if you are, of course). You could, for example, mention such things as holding a clean driving licence, or being qualified to give first aid. Allow it to be seen that you're an interesting person. Make it so that people want to know *more* about what turns you on. This helps to pave the way towards interview questions that you will *enjoy* answering, and will answer *well*.

12. **Make it look well organized.** If your CV is a neat, unfussy, well laid-out document (with careful attention having been paid to spelling, punctuation, grammar and so on), you're likely to make a good impression just from its appearance, quite apart from its content. Get help, if you need it, with the spelling, grammar and punctuation. Print out or photocopy drafts, and get people whose judgement you value to scribble onto these copies any corrections, adjustments or suggestions for making it better. The more feedback you can get, the better your CV will become.

13. **Update your CV regularly.** Your qualifications will continue to change. Your experience and career aims will develop. Your contact details will change from time to time. It's really useful to have an up-to-date CV you can simply print

off or pull out of a drawer, to pop it in an envelope with a
short covering letter expressing your interest in a job you
might consider putting in a formal application for shortly.

14. **Always keep at least one clean copy, and a back-up disk.**
Sometimes, you may want to send off a copy of your CV when
you're really busy – perhaps in the middle of exams. It can be
useful to be able to get out such a copy wherever you are,
whether at home, college, or on placement.

15. **Consider tweaking your CV for particular applications.**
Depending upon what's being asked for in particular job
specifications, you may want to make more – or less – of
particular elements of your history and experience. With a
word-processed CV on disk, it can be relatively easy to print off
a fine-tuned version to go with a particular application. But
don't forget to keep a copy of exactly which version you sent –
it could be weeks or months later that you're invited for
interview, and then you'll need to remind yourself of *exactly*
what you told this firm or organization about yourself.

16. **Add your referees, on a separate sheet.** Sometimes you'll
just want to send a copy of your CV along with an expression
of interest in a job. At other times, you'll want to send it along
with an application form where you've already written the
names and contact details of two or three referees. Sometimes
you may want to use *different* referees for a particular
application than the ones you would normally add to your CV.
Sometimes you'll want your CV to be complete in itself, along
with those referees. All this boils down to *not* fixing your
referees directly into your CV; it's better if they make up the
last sheet of your CV when needed. Referees are important –
so important that the next set of tips is all about them!

Choosing and Using Your Referees

Sometimes, your referees will be contacted as a matter of course when you apply for a job. Alternatively, they may only be contacted when you've got over the first hurdle and been placed on the interview shortlist. In either case, you're unlikely to be offered a job if anything at all goes wrong with your references. The following tips will help you to minimize the possibility of anything going wrong, and also should maximize the value of your references.

1. **Why do employers need you to have referees?** For a start, they need to know that you are who you say you are, and that your details of qualifications and experience are genuine. Moreover, referees are usually asked about whether you are trustworthy and reliable, and whether you get on well with other people. Furthermore, they're often asked whether, in their opinion, you are a suitable candidate for the particular job in question.

2. **Why do *you* need referees?** They can be really helpful in giving you their views about whether a particular application is a good idea in the first place. They may be able to prime you about the sort of qualities that a particular firm or organization is likely to be looking for in applicants. They may be willing to look quickly over your applications and CV, and offer suggestions for making these better. They themselves are likely to have had a lot of experience at applying for jobs themselves, and handling interviews successfully.

3. **Ask your referees for their permission *first*!** Always seek

their permission to use them as referees. And continue to keep them updated about where you've applied to using them as referees. A request for a reference about you should never come as an unwelcome surprise to them – that wouldn't do your reference any good, would it!

4. **At least *one* of your referees should know you well *now*.** While you're a student, this usually means that this referee should be a lecturer or tutor who knows your recent work, and rates it highly.

5. **Another referee needs to be someone who can say favourable things about your character.** This could be someone you've known for longer, and who is in a good position to attest to your personal integrity, trustworthiness and social ability.

6. **Don't forget that referees are *busy* people.** So be careful with their time. Make it as easy as possible for them to write a reference for you when asked. For a start, it's far easier for them to write your reference when they have in front of them a copy of your CV and/or application itself. They then know what *you* have said about yourself, and are able to corroborate your story. Put it the other way – if they *don't* know what you've said about yourself, their references could be *at odds with* your story – not wise!

7. **Choose *authoritative* referees.** Your referees, either because of their qualifications or their professional standing, need to appear on paper to be well-qualified and respectable people, whose word about you can be trusted.

8. **Choose *reliable* referees.** They need to be people who will get down straight away to writing you a reference – or who will get on the phone to provide one to employers verbally if time scales are really tight. If no reference is forthcoming by the date when it's needed, employers may well assume that the referee concerned would not in fact be very supportive regarding your application.

9. **Choose *experienced* referees.** They need to be practised at giving references – they need to know the things employers are looking for in references.

10. **Choose *favourable* referees.** They need, of course, to be favourably disposed towards you – you need an *unfavourable*

referee like you need toothache! You can usually gauge how favourable they are likely to be when you ask their permission. Anyone who's not keen to give you a good reference is likely to be a little hesitant about agreeing to be a referee for you in the first place.

11. **Make sure your referees are *contactable*.** Names (and qualifications), addresses, phone numbers, fax numbers if you can get them, and so on are needed. If a company or organization *doesn't* hear from one or more of your referees, it's often assumed that they don't *want* to give you a reference, and that they may not think you're a worthy applicant! All of this can happen just because you didn't get their address or phone number right!

12. **Double-check any email details you use.** For example, send the referee a short email, for example: 'I'd be very grateful if I could use your name as referee for my application to . . . Is this OK please?' and make sure that the address works. Some referees will read their emails every day – others don't!

13. **Double-check phone or fax numbers.** The problem with faxes in particular is that if a machine somewhere in the world *receives* the fax, it's usually assumed it's gone to the right person. Sometimes it hasn't! It only takes one digit in the number to be wrong and it could be anyone who puts the request for your reference into the bin!

14. **Be particularly careful with names and addresses too.** There could be five people called 'Dr Jones' at your institution. If the request for your reference arrives on the desk of the Dr Jones who is away on a year's research in the Far East, you won't get a reference! Postal mail often goes to the wrong people in institutions.

15. **Keep your referees *informed*.** It doesn't take long to drop a line, or an email, or a quick phone call to each referee you use, *each time* you use them. Then at least they know which jobs you've gone in for. They may, indeed, let you know about similar job advertisements they happen to notice.

16. **Continue to thank your referees.** Even if you've got their permission, you might be using their support on several quite different occasions. You can couple your continued thanks to your letters or phone calls keeping them informed.

Application Forms

When you're applying for jobs, you are likely to fill in dozens of these, perhaps hundreds during your life. However, you'll only be invited to a small fraction of interviews. Another way of looking at it is that you're likely to have to get through completing quite a few application forms for every interview opportunity. But whether or not you get called for interview (let alone get the job) depends, to at least some extent, on how well you go about the application form in the first place. So it's worth getting to know how to handle application forms well, and quickly, and efficiently.

1. **Your application form should become your ambassador.** It gives people an overall impression of *you* – and for obvious reasons you want to make that a *good* impression.
2. **Sometimes, your application form will be your *only* chance to impress.** You might often be asked to include your CV (curriculum vitae) *as well as* a completed application form, but sometimes it's only the application form that will be considered in the shortlisting process.
3. **Have all the information that you will need for application forms in one place.** If you've already made a CV, and kept it up to date, you're winning here. Most of the routine or factual information that you'll need for application forms will be in your CV. It will contain all the important dates, addresses, referees, and so on. In any case, it's worth having an up-to-date CV ready and waiting on your computer (or safely stored already printed out in a drawer) at all times, and sending a copy in with each application, even when you're not *asked* to send a CV. In fact the *only* time not to send in a CV along with a job application is if instructed 'Don't send a CV'!
4. **Make sure there are no discrepancies between the detail on your application form and that in your CV.** For example, if dates or qualifications or addresses are different between the two, the impression that is created is of someone who is not well organized – and possibly untruthful.
5. **Sometimes you'll be able to fill in application forms online.** This has pros and cons. An advantage is that you can usually put as much as you want into a 'box' – the box expands as you type things into it. A disadvantage, however, is that you may not be able to see how the whole thing will appear on paper. Nor can you bring any second thoughts into play if you've already 'sent' it electronically.
6. **Make at least one photocopy of the blank application form.** It's not usually possible to sit and fill in such forms without at least some planning. You may need to find out how much information you can comfortably squeeze into some of the boxes. Keep the real form for when you've finished experimenting.

7. **Watch for instructions such as 'use black ink'.** Most completed application forms will be photocopied at the other end, and circulated to a panel of people who will agree on the candidates to be shortlisted for interview. If you use any *other* colour than black, it might not photocopy well, and then your application is at a disadvantage already. Furthermore, you may be branded at their end as 'Doesn't follow instructions!'

8. **Sometimes you may even be instructed 'don't type'.** There may be specific instructions that the application should be handwritten (in black ink, of course!). There is a long history of some companies and organizations using 'graphologists' (people who analyse handwriting) to work out the likely characteristics of applicants just from their handwriting! Whether this is a science or an art – or a con – it happens. In these circumstances, at least write neatly enough to be easily legible.

9. **Use your form to create the impression that you're a well-organized person.** One way of doing this is to make sure that your form doesn't have crossings-out or information spilling out of a box. Don't cover it with white correction fluid either.

10. **Use your form to show that you're a stickler for detail.** For example, when listing your qualifications, give the dates of each of these, along with the name of the examining body, as well as the grades or marks you were awarded, and so on. Give postcodes with addresses, and telephone numbers for anyone they may wish to contact (your present institution, present or past employers, referees, and so on). Where you know fax numbers or email addresses, put these in too.

11. **Fit your information to the sizes of the boxes.** Don't put too much into a small box. Edit your information down in such circumstances. You can always write 'For further information, please see enclosed CV.'

12. **Try to avoid too much 'blank space'.** If there's *nothing* you can put into a particular box, you're stuck with that. But if there's *something* you can put into a rather large box, expand upon it a bit, so that it looks more substantial. Don't just *write* big, however!

13. **Don't *just* write 'Please see enclosed CV'!** If you simply

refer to your CV instead of being bothered to do the application form justice, they're likely to think 'Here is someone who couldn't be bothered to fill in the application form' and that's likely to be the end of your chance of being shortlisted.

14. **Make the most of responsibilities you've held.** There's usually somewhere on an application form where you can make it clear that you're the kind of person who has held positions of trust (for example been Treasurer of a club or society), or that you've been responsible for supervising other people, and so on.

15. **Make the most of being a sociable person.** Employers *like* people who are going to be able to get on with other people. So don't present yourself through the detail you include on your application form as being a hermit or a recluse. But don't go *too* far! Don't come across as *only* being able to function as a human being in the company of other people – include some things that show you can indeed work on your own too.

16. **Plant some interview questions!** This is easier to do than you might think. For example, if the details you happen to give about your hobbies or leisure activities look *interesting* to the interview panel, someone is likely to ask you to talk about them. The more you can talk at an interview about things you *know* well, and *like* a lot, the more air time you'll have to give the panel a positive overall impression.

17. **'Why should we appoint *you*?'** There's occasionally a direct question along these lines. 'What would you bring to the post?' is another way this could be asked. Don't be too modest in such circumstances. It's perfectly acceptable to reply along the lines of: 'I believe I have just the right amount of experience to do this job well' or 'I believe that I can bring some flair and initiative, while still being quick to tune in to the situation around me.'

18. **Fill in the *real* form carefully and neatly.** If you've used your copies to practise what you're going to include on the final version you send in, it should not take too long to finish it off.

19. **Keep a photocopy of the final completed form.** If you're

selected for interview, it is really useful to remind yourself of *exactly* what you said on that particular form – you might have completed ten others since you wrote it. At least some of the interview questions will be based on what you wrote on the form.

20.   **Include a 'letter of application' along with your application form and CV.** Normally this only needs to be a short letter, along the lines of: 'Please find enclosed my application for the post of (whatever it is) at (whoever the company is) advertised in (where you saw the advert)', along with your name, address and contact details. Occasionally, however, you could be asked to 'write a letter of application' *instead of* filling in an application form or sending a CV. There are more suggestions about this sort of application in the next set of tips.

Writing a *Letter* of Application

As mentioned at the end of the previous set of tips on 'Application Forms', you may sometimes be asked to apply for a job by 'letter of application'. This, as you will see, is somewhat different. In such cases, there is no 'best' way of going about it, but the following tips should help you to make such a letter fit for the purpose.

1. **Look carefully at the instructions.** Play detective! Work out everything you can from the instructions about what they may be looking for in a letter of application. Some things are fairly obvious. They will need to find out from your letter most of the answers to the 'hidden' questions asked below.
2. **What's this letter then?** Start purposefully, just as you would if you were writing a short letter to accompany a completed application form. Make it clear in your first paragraph that the purpose of this letter is that you're wishing to be considered in connection with the appointment (whatever it is) at (wherever it is), which came to your attention (however it did), and that you are pleased to submit for their consideration the following letter of application for this post.
3. **Who are you?** As with an application form, it is normal to say a bit about your education, qualifications and experience. In a letter of application, it can be useful to relate this directly to the roles or duties of the particular post for which you're applying.

4. **Where do you live, how can you be contacted, and so on?** Most of this information can be given as your letterhead, at the top of your letter. It is, however, important to make sure that they *can* contact you – if they want to invite you to interview, for example.

5. **Why are you interested in this particular post?** It is useful to give the impression that this isn't just another random shot-in-the-dark application, but that you're really interested in what you already know about the post in question, and eager to find out yet more (at an interview, for example).

6. **What relevant experience and expertise can you bring to the post?** This is where you need to blow your own trumpet – but not *too* loudly. Look carefully at what's most relevant to the post from your existing educational experience. Also think about what you expect to have gained by the time you finish the course you're currently studying. In addition, think of any *other* experience, possibly from previous part-time or full-time employment, or associated with your hobbies and leisure activities. Make the most of any sensible connections between such experience and the nature of the post you're applying for.

7. **What particular strengths could you bring to the post?** Again, blow your own trumpet – preferably where you can add a 'for example . . .' sentence or two to *support* your claims about yourself.

8. **What would you be hoping for, if appointed to this post?** This is your chance to expand on *why* you are interested in the post, and to be rather more specific regarding your own hopes or expectations of the post.

9. **Apart from your studies, what makes you tick?** They would not ask the question quite like this on an application form, but this is likely to be an aspect of your life they would want to find out about.

10. **Who can vouch for you?** It's useful to include here the same sorts of detail as you would have given under 'Referees' in a normal application form, or along with your CV.

11. **Then end with a good final sentence or two.** This is another of those times when it's really useful to make

a good *last* impression. In particular, you want whoever reads your letter to be *interested* in finding out more about you. This is what could lead them to shortlist you for interview.

Preparing for an Interview

Some people thrive on interviews. If you're such a person, you probably won't need any of the tips that follow. Other people, however, *hate* interviews. If you're in this club, the following suggestions may help you to prepare for them in ways that will improve your chances when you get there, and help you to hate them less.

1. **Congratulate yourself.** Being asked to go for an interview is already an achievement. Many other people won't have got so far. If you're asked for interview, you're already in with a chance.
2. **But keep it in perspective.** Yes, you've got a chance, but statistically it may be a one-in-three chance at best, perhaps as low as one in ten. It could be even lower, if for one reason or another they're already got a particular candidate in mind – for example a 'known quantity', someone who has already been doing the job for a while.
3. **Get practised.** The more often you're interviewed, the better you'll become at it. Use friends, fellow students, relatives, anyone. Become practised at answering questions on the spot. You won't become good at being interviewed just by reading about it, it's something you learn by doing it. These tips can help you to find out *how* to go about it all, but only you can practise till you're good at it.
4. **Remember that interviews are not just for getting jobs.** There are all sorts of other circumstances where being good at being interviewed is an asset for you. These include

talking to professional people as a client – for example doctors, dentists, counsellors, lawyers, customer-care personnel, complaints officers, police officers, travel consultants, bank managers, sales personnel, and so on. In all such cases, they will want to find out things from you, and you will want something from them.

5. **Practise *not* getting tense.** Take the view that each and every interview is a useful learning experience – whether or not it gets you the job you're after. It's best if you can be so laid-back about it that if they offer you the job you can regard it as a bonus rather than a right. When you're so relaxed, you're more likely to be offered the job in any case.

6. **Prepare for 'Tell us a little about yourself.'** Almost all interviews start rather like this. Practise explaining your background, experience and so on. Rehearse this until you can keep going for as long as five minutes if you need to – you'll usually be interrupted long before then.

7. **Don't bank on people having picked everything up from your application.** Not every interviewer will have read everything you sent to them. Don't just say 'as I explained in my application . . .'. Even if they *have* read it all, they may want you to explain yourself in your own words.

8. **Do your research.** Find out what you can about the firm or organization you're applying to. You'll often have a wealth of information sent to you. There may well be a website to explore. It's useful to be in the position of being able to ask sensible, informed questions yourself, at some point in the interview. 'I saw from your website that . . .', followed by a question, shows that you're interested.

9. **Find out whether you may be asked to give a short presentation.** Sometimes, shortlisted candidates are asked to prepare one, for example outlining what they in particular can bring to the post in question. If this *is* part of the picture, the tips elsewhere in this book on preparing and giving presentations should be useful to you.

10. **Prepare for 'Why should we offer this post to *you*?'** Be prepared to blow your own trumpet in a quiet but firm way then. Don't be embarrassed about your expertise, experience and strengths. Don't underplay your hand.

11. **Look back to your application form.** Before setting out for the interview, dig out your copy of the application form you sent, and the letter of application you composed, and the particular edition of your CV you supplied. This is what they have at their end – and is probably *all* that they know about you so far, apart perhaps from one or two references. Many of the interview questions will be based on what *you* revealed about the sort of person you are, and your background and experience.

12. **Dress for the occasion.** Use your judgement. Remember how important first impressions can be. It's usually better to be a little over-formal than under-formal for interviews (but there are exceptions). If you can, build in a little leeway to 'dress up' or 'dress down' when you get there, perhaps when you see what most of the other candidates are wearing.

13. **Get there early.** Plan extra time for your journey. It's not a

good idea to arrive breathless and flustered. Imagine the mental energy you'd dissipate if you'd spent half an hour *knowing* you were going to be late!

14. **Keep your travel receipts.** Usually you can claim your travel expenses back, if you're offered the job and take it, or even if you are not offered the job. If you're offered the job and *turn it down* you may not be able to claim your expenses back, however.

15. **Use the spare time you've built in when you arrive.** Look around. Talk to anyone who's willing to tell you more about the organization you're applying to join. Listen, rather than talk. You may find out more about whether you *really* want the job or not. You may also find out some questions *you* can ask about the organization.

16. **Be ready for anything!** You may have one-to-one informal chats, informal group discussions, one-to-one formal interviews, or even a formal panel interview with perhaps a dozen people behind the table. You may be given psychometric tests or other exercises. Even when you meet something completely unexpected, regard it as a chance to develop your experience of being interviewed – even if it won't pay off on this particular occasion.

Giving a Good Interview

The next set of suggestions is for when you arrive, from even before you walk in, until the interview is over. It's all common sense, but if you're naturally a bit tense, you may need to think consciously about it.

1. **Be polite to everyone!** Even before the interview itself starts, you'll talk to people. You may not know exactly who they are. The most important-*looking* person around may not be the most important person in the context of your particular interview.
2. **Don't let other candidates put you off.** Sometimes, candidates seem to engage in a war of nerves, hoping to damage each other's chances. Don't even be part of this; there could well be someone quietly *noticing* how candidates behave with each other before the interview.
3. **On entering, take your time!** Don't just rush to the empty chair and sit on it. Soon enough, you'll be motioned to where they want you, and invited to take your seat.
4. **Make the most of eye contact.** If looking people in the eye makes you feel uncomfortable, practise till you can *appear* to be doing so, but actually blurring your vision slightly, or looking just past them. It's rather the same skill as looking a camera in the eye – you can't make *real* eye contact with a camera, but you can *appear* to do so. Anyone can develop their eye-contact skills with practice.
5. **Smile.** Don't, of course, wear a fixed, maniacal grin! But

smiles are infectious, and you'll often find that when you smile at someone who's just asked you a question, you strike up at least some rapport with them. When you first go in, it does no harm to accompany your smile with a 'good morning' or 'good afternoon' and so on, being careful, of course, not to say the wrong one.

6.   **Try to *appear* alert and confident – even when you're anything but!** Most performers on live TV or stage shows *look* calm and unflustered – but most will admit that their pulse rate is up by quite a bit each time, until they get into their stride. Yet they put on a good act of looking calm, and so can you, with practice.

7.   **Speak slowly, calmly and low.** Some of the credit is attached to giving calm and confident answers, and some for giving *good* answers. Don't miss out on the 'calm and confident' bit, and just give good answers!

8.   **Don't lose your ends!** When people are nervous, they often drop their voices towards the end of a sentence, and naturally the meaning doesn't get across as well as it would have done if they'd kept up the voice all the way. The ending of something you're saying is important, as it is the natural trigger for the next question.

9.   **Try to avoid silence.** In general, periods of silence during an interview are bad things. Try to have something to say, or something to ask, whenever a silence seems to be getting a little too long. But remember that what *to you* seems like a long silence may only be quite a short one – your impression of time could be distorted by nerves.

10. **Don't interrupt anyone.** Don't keep speaking when someone is trying to ask you something or clarifying a point for you. If there is something you are desperate to tell your interviewers – or to ask them – wait, there will be another chance for you to do so soon enough.

11. **Don't bluff.** When you don't know something, it's usually far safer to admit it straight away, than to be found out after you've spouted a good deal of nonsense. 'I'm sorry but I've not come across this yet' is better than saying something silly in reply to a question.

12. **Seek clarification of a question, when necessary.** Don't

just ask for it to be repeated, however. Offer *your* interpretation back to the questioner, perhaps asking 'Is *this* what you'd like me to explain?' This can give you a little longer to get your answer thought through but, more importantly, it helps you to make sure that you're homing in on what they're asking you.

13. **Don't be put off by people making notes.** In particular, resist the temptation to stare at what they're writing in order to try and make out what they've put down. In any case, they could be writing *good* things down about your interview – so don't assume that everything they take down will be used *against* you as evidence.

14. **Make the most of *your* air time.** Talk convincingly about the things you *do* know. For example, when you're talking about *your* interests or hobbies, you're on home ground, and you'll almost certainly know more about these than anyone else in the room. Use such opportunities to show your interviewers how you can be confident and enthused. This impression may carry over and compensate for some of the things you're not so confident about.

15. **At panel interviews, talk to *everyone*.** Don't just reply to the person who asked you the last question. That person will probably *know* whether you're giving a good answer or not, but other people might not, and you may be able to convince *them* that you're giving a strong answer even when you're struggling a bit. If you can impress most of the panel for most of the time, you're giving a good interview.

16. **Try to make a good *last* impression.** It's important that your interview doesn't just fizzle out. There's sometimes what seems like a long silence at the end of an interview, particularly a panel interview, when no one has any further questions to ask you. Have one or two questions ready to ask *them*, if and when you're invited to do so.

17. **Ask sensible questions.** Don't ask about pay, conditions, holidays and so on. It's better to ask about training opportunities, and better still to follow through by asking them about things that *they* seem to be proud of, or keen on. What might they *like* you to ask? What would give them *pleasure* in explaining to you?

After an Interview

If you got what you wanted from the interview, you won't feel the need for any suggestions on how to cope with the result. But, statistically, *most* interviews don't get candidates what they were hoping for. The learning experience can continue to be built upon, however, and that's what the following suggestions focus on most.

1. **If they offer you the job, the best thing is to accept it!** Sometimes at the end of an interview, they will ask 'If we were to offer you the job now, *would* you accept it?' If you say 'No thanks', that is, of course, the end of the story regarding that particular job. That indeed may be what you really mean, and if so, that's fine. But saying 'yes' can open the door to further negotiation, if that is needed.
2. **Keep your referees informed – and thanked.** Whether you've got the job or not, your referees still need to be thanked – you will almost certainly need at least one of them again sooner or later. Your referees may also be able to give you further advice if you weren't successful on that particular occasion. For example, *they* may have been asked particular questions about you, which told them a lot more about the sort of candidate that was being sought on that occasion.
3. **If you *have* been successful, look back at why.** It's still worthwhile to reflect on the interview, and work out what went well. It certainly won't be your *last* interview, and the same things may be worth building on in the future. What was

your best moment in the interview? Which answer were you particularly proud of giving? Although the remainder of the suggestions below apply to interviews that didn't get you the job, it's still worth reflecting on at least some of these if you *did* get it.

4. **If you were not offered the job, keep your spirits up.** Remind yourself that *most* candidates don't get offered the job. To have got to interview stage, you've already done better than many applicants. You were at least deemed to be *appointable* on paper at that stage in your application.

5. **The successful candidate could indeed have been more suitable.** That doesn't mean this person is a better human being than you are – it could simply be the case that he or she had experience or expertise that was more closely connected to the person specification for that particular job.

6. **Continue to regard it as a useful learning experience.** It may have been a disappointing one for you, but that doesn't make the learning associated with it any less valuable to you.

7. **Don't overdo the post-mortem.** While it's useful to reflect on what went well, and what didn't go so well, don't 'replay the tape' ad nauseam. Resist the temptation to think 'If only I'd said such-and-such' or 'If only I had known the answer to so-and-so'. What's past is past, but there will be a next time. It won't be the same job in the same place – but it could indeed be a better job in a better place next time. Turn each 'If only I had . . .' into 'Next time, I'll try to . . .' and then let it go.

8. **Do jot down any questions that caused you trouble.** You may well be asked similar questions in future, and forewarned is forearmed. In fact, interviews are the best possible way of finding out more about what you will need to know on future occasions.

9. **Don't forget to think about the parts of the interview where you *were* doing well.** Build on the experience. Think back to where you were most confident. Think back to the questions you found to be perfectly straightforward to answer.

10. **Take any opportunity you can to gain feedback about the interview.** For example, you may be able to find out a little more by telephoning and asking for feedback. You can do this by letter too, but if they will give you feedback over the

phone you've got additional clues from tone of voice and so on. You could indeed ask whether they would be prepared to offer you any advice about future applications you may make. Sometimes you will learn a lot from this. They may even tell you what lost you that particular job, but more often they will tell you a little about the things that swung the balance in favour of the successful candidate. Any of this is useful knowledge for next time.

11. **Resist any temptation to defend yourself when receiving feedback.** Once a decision is made, there's no mileage in trying to make up for lost ground. Indeed, if you try to justify your own candidature at this stage, you'll simply stem the flow of feedback. So just listen, and ask gentle probing questions so that you can learn as much as you can from the occasion.

Final Words

I didn't want to end this book by just stopping after the tips on interviews. You'll need to continue to be an effective learner all through your career.

The better you become at learning, the more you'll enjoy life. The whole of life can be regarded as a learning experience, and most people continue to need to learn new things.

Moreover, being a good learner allows you to make and take all sorts of opportunities, and meet challenges head on through your career. You can also help other people around you to become better at learning, and more successful. Few things give greater pleasure than the feeling that one has helped other people to do themselves justice and to succeed.

So don't just leave behind the things you will have learnt by developing your learning tactics at college – take all the best things on with you into the next stage of your life.

Further Reading

Barnes, Rob (1995) *Successful Study for Degrees.* London, UK: Routledge.

Bell, Judith (1993) *Doing your Research Project.* Buckingham, UK: Open University Press.

Chambers, E. and Northedge, A. (1997) *The Arts Good Study Guide.* Milton Keynes, UK: Open University Worldwide.

Creme, Phyllis and Lea, Mary R. (1997) *Writing at University: A Guide for Students.* Buckingham, UK: Open University Press.

Cryer, Pat (1996) *The Research Student's Guide to Success.* Buckingham, UK: Open University Press.

Fairbairn, Gavin J. and Winch, Christopher (1996) *Reading, Writing and Reasoning: A Guide for Students*, 2nd edn. Buckingham, UK: Open University Press.

Northedge, Andy (1990) *The Good Study Guide.* Milton Keynes, UK: Open University Worldwide.

Northedge, A., Thomas, J., Lane, A. and Peasgood, A. (1997) *The Sciences Good Study Guide.* Milton Keynes, UK: Open University Worldwide.

Race, Phil (1999) *How to Get a Good Degree.* Buckingham, UK: Open University Press.

Race, Phil (2000) *How to Win as a Final-Year Student.* Buckingham, UK: Open University Press.

Saunders, Danny (ed.) (1994) *The Complete Student Handbook.* Oxford, UK: Blackwell.

Index